Mexico's Criminal Insurgency

A Small Wars Journal—El Centro Anthology

John P. Sullivan and Robert J. Bunker
Primary Authors

iUniverse, Inc.
Bloomington

Mexico's Criminal Insurgency
A Small Wars Journal—El Centro Anthology

iUniverse books may be ordered through booksellers or by contacting:

iUniverse
1663 Liberty Drive
Bloomington, IN 47403
www.iuniverse.com
1-800-Authors (1-800-288-4677)

ISBN: 978-1-4759-2729-0 (sc)
ISBN: 978-1-4759-2730-6 (ebk)

Printed in the United States of America

iUniverse rev. date: 5/23/2012

ABOUT SMALL WARS JOURNAL
AND FOUNDATION

SMALL WARS JOURNAL FACILITATES the exchange of information among practitioners, thought leaders, and students of Small Wars, in order to advance knowledge and capabilities in the field. We hope this, in turn, advances the practice and effectiveness of those forces prosecuting Small Wars in the interest of self-determination, freedom, and prosperity for the population in the area of operations.

We believe that Small Wars are an enduring feature of modern politics. We do not believe that true effectiveness in Small Wars is a 'lesser included capability' of a force tailored for major theater war. And we never believed that 'bypass built-up areas' was a tenable position warranting the doctrinal primacy it has held for too long— this site is an evolution of the MOUT Homepage, Urban Operations Journal, and urbanoperations.com, all formerly run by the *Small Wars Journal's* Editor-in-Chief.

The characteristics of Small Wars have evolved since the Banana Wars and Gunboat Diplomacy. War is never purely military, but today's Small Wars are even less pure with the greater inter-connectedness of the 21st century. Their conduct typically involves the projection and employment of the full spectrum of national and coalition power by a broad community of practitioners. The military is still generally the biggest part of the pack, but there a lot of other wolves. The strength of the pack is the wolf, and the strength of the wolf is the pack.

The *Small Wars Journal's* founders come from the Marine Corps. Like Marines deserve to be, we are very proud of this; we are also conscious and cautious of it. This site seeks to transcend any viewpoint that is single service, and any that is purely military or naively U.S.-centric. We pursue a comprehensive approach to Small Wars, integrating the full joint, allied, and coalition military with their governments' federal or national agencies, non-governmental agencies, and private organizations. Small Wars are big undertakings, demanding a coordinated effort from a huge community of interest.

We thank our contributors for sharing their knowledge and experience, and hope you will continue to join us as we build a resource for our community of interest to engage in a professional dialog on this painfully relevant topic. Share your thoughts, ideas, successes, and mistakes; make us all stronger.

"...I know it when I see it."

"Small Wars" is an imperfect term used to describe a broad spectrum of spirited continuation of politics by other means, falling somewhere in the middle bit of the continuum between feisty diplomatic words and global thermonuclear war. The Small Wars Journal embraces that imperfection.

Just as friendly fire isn't, there isn't necessarily anything small about a Small War.

The term "Small War" either encompasses or overlaps with a number of familiar terms such as counterinsurgency, foreign internal defense, support and stability operations, peacemaking, peacekeeping, and many flavors of intervention. Operations such as noncombatant evacuation, disaster relief, and humanitarian assistance will often either be a part of a Small War, or have a Small Wars feel to them. Small Wars involve a wide spectrum of specialized tactical, technical, social, and cultural skills and expertise, requiring great ingenuity from their practitioners. The *Small Wars Manual* (a wonderful resource, unfortunately more often referred to than read) notes that:

Small Wars demand the highest type of leadership directed by intelligence, resourcefulness, and ingenuity. Small Wars are conceived in uncertainty, are conducted often with precarious responsibility and doubtful authority, under indeterminate orders lacking specific instructions.

The "three block war" construct employed by General Krulak is exceptionally useful in describing the tactical and operational challenges of a Small War and of many urban operations. Its only shortcoming is that is so useful that it is often mistaken as a definition or as a type of operation.

• • •

Small Wars Journal is NOT a government, official, or big corporate site. It is run by Small Wars Foundation, a 501(c)(3) non-profit corporation, for the benefit of the Small Wars community of interest. The site principals are Dave Dilegge (Editor-in-Chief), Bill Nagle (Publisher), Robert Haddick (Managing Editor) and Peter Munson (Editor). Dilegge, Nagle and Haddick, along with Daniel Kelly, serve as the Small Wars Foundation Board of Directors.

Contents

FOREWORD: MEXICO'S CRIMINAL INSURGENCY AND SWJ EL CENTRO

Dave Dilegge
March 2012

THIS WORK IS NOT only the first publication of a *Small Wars Journal* anthology but also celebrates the establishment of the *SWJ El Centro* forum. Contained within it are cutting edge articles pertaining to the criminal insurgency taking place in Mexico—essentially the 21ˢᵗ century equivalent of the small wars of the last century but undertaken by criminal organizations, both hierarchical and networked in form, rather than by traditional Maoist-like insurgents. Additional works will certainly be produced concerning this pivotal security threat to the United States and her Latin American allies as the study of the criminal insurgencies taking place in the Western Hemisphere becomes more organized and systematic under the *El Centro Fellows program*.

What has been confounding for some *SWJ* readers is our embrace of this topic as a *"cause célèbre"* since about 2008. While most eyes in the insurgency studies profession remained firmly fixed on Iraq and Afghanistan, a small yet growing group of authors have been concerned with the developing cartel and gang threat in Mexico and in other regions of Latin America. For John Sullivan and Robert Bunker, their initial gang and cartel research dates back to the mid-to-late 1990s. What many still have not grasped is that cartels, gangs, and other criminal organizations can become politicized either by purpose and intent or accidentally (*de facto*) with the capture of a town or city. Many of these organizations may have initially only sought governmental non-interference with their illicit narcotic and other criminal pursuits in order to operate with impunity in the territories that they held. The end result is the same though. Behind the façade of legitimate authority is that of one cartel or another wearing a 'bloody mask', whether it is the Gulf, Zetas, Sinaloa, La Familia, Juarez, or any of a number of other criminal organizations. With economic and military (cartel gunman) power comes political power. The cartels and paramilitaries in some cities and regions have even evolved to the point where they tax the local population, viewing themselves as benefactors offering basic services, protection, and spiritual guidance. What we are witnessing in Mexico is a fusion of local warlordism and social banditry, expanding criminal enterprise and parastate emergence— an insurgency fostered by both secular criminality and narco spirituality.

The authors in this work have been investigating the evolution of criminal insurgencies, the crime-war overlap, the barbarization of the conflict, new forms of spirituality—including Santa Muerte ritualistic killings— third generations gangs, and cartel information operations (info ops) for some years now. They have also provided us with useful tools such as new strategic perspectives, web and social media resources, and differing views on the conflict in Mexico from divergent fields of security studies. Their contribution to this field of study should not be downplayed; beyond their significant contributions to *Small Wars Journal*, they have also gone on to produce other important works that have begun to influence Washington perceptions, policy formulation, and decision making and have also greatly influenced the scholarly literature in the areas of US national security policy, Mexican security, transnational organized crime and in gang and cartel studies.

In sum, this anthology represents some of the best and brightest scholars of today who are writing on the evolving security environment in Mexico and the implications this may hold for the United States. They have greatly enhanced our understanding of crime wars and criminal insurgencies—21st century war and conflict waged by non-state entities— and the impact this new form of warfare is having on states. For this, we embrace them and have established the new *SWJ El Centro* forum found at http://smallwarsjournal.com/elcentro to further promote their professionalism and scholarship.

PREFACE:
A SINALOAN KINGPIN, A REPORTER, AND THE REALITY OF MEXICAN STATE SOVEREIGNTY

Max G. Manwaring[1]

Excerpt derived from
"A 'New' Dynamic in the Western Hemisphere Security Environment."
Initially published in September 2009

The preface to John Sullivan and Robert Bunker's *Small Wars Journal-El Centro* anthology on *Mexico's Criminal Insurgency* provides rich context concerning rising cartel influence in that nation. It was originally slated to appear in the *Narcos Over the Border* (Routledge) edited work but was not published due to space limitations. This essay is still highly relevant because "El Chapo", a Sinaloan Kingpin, figures prominently in this essay and still garners headlines. Essentially he is now considered—as of March 2012— to be more powerful than the Colombian drug lord Pablo Escobar was during the 1980s according to a senior US Drug Enforcement Administration official.[2]

This vignette, taken from a very interesting and instructive article written by Guy Lawson,[3] is an attempt to capture the essence of the article. The intent here, however, is to briefly examine contemporary sociopolitical life in Sinaloa with a critical eye on the reality of effective state sovereignty.

The Individual Being Interviewed: Juaquin Guzman Loera, better known as "El Chapo" (Shorty). El Chapo controls a Sinaloa Cartel that controls the Arizona border towns of Nogales and Mexicali. He has opposition, however. First, there are erstwhile friends who have developed a personal feud with El Chapo that seems to go on and on and become more and more violent. These antagonists are two brothers, Mochomo (Red Ant) and Barbas (the Beard), who are leaders of the Beltran Leyva cartel. Then there are the seemingly ever-present Zetas agents trying to expand their own and the Gulf Cartel's illegal drug routes into the United States. The Gulf Cartel and the Zetas appear to have teamed together with Mochomo and Barbas in an attempt to eliminate El Chapo from the market.

In the capital of the Mexican state of Sinaloa, Culiacan, El Chapo is known as "a kind of folk hero— part Robin Hood, part Billy the Kid." He has more money, more women, and more weapons than any other TCO in the area—except the Zetas. Because El Chapo is relatively generous with some (actually, very little) of his money, people "respect him." He grew up poor, planting corn and marijuana. Over time, he built massive underground tunnels to smuggle cocaine into Arizona, and he subsequently assembled a fleet of boats, trucks, and aircraft that made him one of the most wanted drug dealers in the world. And, he now— among other things—finances new entrepreneurs as they grow both marijuana and poppies for heroin. El Chapo, however, is most famous for his "miraculous escape" from a federal prison in 2001 just before he was to be extradited to the United States for trial on US drug charges. "He had a plush suite in prison, complete with a personal chef, plenty of whisky, an endless supply of Viagra, and a girlfriend called Zulema." The common wisdom is that El Chapo gave all that up to go back to Sinaloa and help out his friends and neighbors.

Moreover, the people of Sinaloa are convinced that the federal government in Mexico City let El Chapo escape because he is the only drug lord who has the resources and intelligence to face up to the other cartels and to the Zetas.[4] The argument, simply put, is that the federal government cannot do much. The police are incompetent and corrupt; laws constrain government, while a TCO can do whatever it wants; and regular army troops are a poor match for the much better armed, equipped, and trained Zetas. In short, it is better to let the TCOs destroy themselves rather than fight them directly.

…..The State of Sinaloa, Mexico. Sinaloa is a small state on the Mexican Pacific coast across the Gulf of California from the Baja California peninsula. It is situated between the sea and the almost impassable Sierra Madre Occidental on the east. There are probably not many more than a million inhabitants of the entire state, but an average of three drug-related murders are estimated to take place every day of the year in Sinaloa. That statistic explains the front-page headline of the local newspaper on the day that our American reporter arrived in Culiacan: "Worse Than Iraq."

The Capital City of Culiacan, Sinaloa. That first day in Culiacan, everyone in the city was wondering what El Chapo might do to take revenge for the death of his 20-year-old son a few weeks earlier. The young man was shot and killed in broad daylight during a drive-by attack by 15 gunmen, one of whom fired a bazooka. The murder was attributed to the Beltran-Leyva cartel. Weeks later, four more decapitated bodies were dumped in the center of Culiacan with a note addressed to El Chapo, saying, "You're next." Three days later, three more bodies—this time with legs as well as heads severed—were found. Among them was a former police *comandante.* Within hours, another police officer was shot and killed, along with a companion and a bystander. Within another few days, two more grotesquely decapitated bodies were dumped outside a farm owned by a *capo* (criminal chieftain) allied with El Chapo.

That was just one series of events discussed on that first day in Culiacan. Something less important than the murder of El Chapo's son was also a topic of conversation. Only a few days before the arrival of our reporter, a gang of gunmen pulled up in front of an auto shop in the center of the city. They opened fire with AK-47s and AR-15s. Within minutes, nine people were dead. Then, as the assailants fled along Zapata Boulevard, they gunned down two police officers. On Insurgentes Avenue, the killers opened fire on federal troops stationed outside a judicial building. There was no pursuit and no arrests. All that anyone seemed to know was that the gunmen were after a small time narcotraficante known as "Alligator." A local official succinctly explained, "No one will talk."

As one might have guessed,

Culiacan is a drug-industry town the way Los Angeles is an entertainment town. Every business is connected, directly or indirectly, with illegal drugs. There are narco discos and narco restaurants. In the upscale malls scattered around town, high-end jewelers sell gaudy and expensive necklaces favored by narco wives, and girlfriends, and hookers. Narco chic is Valentino and Moschino pants, ostrich-skin boots, a black belt with a narco nickname (such as 'Alligator') engraved on it, and a Versace hand bag big enough to hold a stash of drugs and cash needed to pay off the police.

Thus, every day, Culiacan stages a sort of ongoing soap opera. But Culiacan is much smaller than Los Angeles. In Culiacan, one can see everyone and everything in one or two episodes.

On the Road and into Tamazula de Victoria. The American reporter was hoping to meet El Chapo and interview him. Through professional connections, he was introduced to "Julio," an opium (poppy) farmer, who considered himself a good friend of El Chapo. He has partied many times with El Chapo and his friends, and El Chapo supplies him with the seeds for the poppies he grows. Julio told the reporter that he could take him to a town called Tamazula where El Chapo lives—"if he isn't in Guatemala or El Salvador."

The highway inland and toward the mountains from Culiacan is dotted by large haciendas (ranches), sheltered behind 30-foot-high walls. Tamazula itself boasts a new school and condo developments—signs of the prosperity bought with narco dollars. In the middle of the village, on a hill overlooking the valley, a mansion stands behind large black steel gates. "At the bottom of the hill, just under the gaze of the narco mansion, there is a kind of contradiction common in the Sierra Madres. It is an army outpost ironically illustrating that the fortunes of the law and outlaws are inextricably entwined." Julio explained that the house belongs to one of El Chapo's allies. But El Chapo is not there, "he is up there, at a ranch of a capo named Nachito." Julio pointed to a rough dirt track that could be seen leading up into the mountains from Tamazula.

On the way out of town and toward the mountains, Julio stopped and ducked into a tiny office to collect the monthly subsidy he receives from the Mexican government for not growing illegal drugs—despite the fact that he does grow opium and marijuana. This is another closely related contradiction and irony in Sinaloa, illustrating the "you leave me alone and I'll leave you alone" armistice that exists between the narcos and the government. A few minutes later, in the distance they spotted what appeared to be a platoon of soldiers. Julio suddenly decided that they should turn around and go back. He insisted that it would be unsafe to go any further. He argued that the armed men could be federal troops, El Chapo's men, *gatilleros* (triggermen) for the Beltran-Leyva cartel, or Zetas. In any case, they would recognize a *gringo* (American) in the car and assume that he was from the U.S. Drug Enforcement Agency (DEA) or U.S. Central Intelligence Agency (CIA). Julio was prickly and insistent: "If you want to find El Chapo, you should look near the village of La Tuna. I know people who can take you there."

On the way back to Culiacan, conversation stayed centered on the inordinately high level of violence and impunity to prosecution for it in Sinaloa. In the capital city, the front page of the newspaper now featured a street-by-street diagram of the most recent beheadings and assassinations: "El Mapa De La Muerte" (the death map).

Our reporter never did find out how the vendetta between El Chapo and Mochomo and Barbas came out. It really did not matter. The back and forth violence continues apace and seems to blur into a deep gray fog. In that fog, the violence between and within the rival cartels, the enforcer gangs, and government forces does not appear likely to end anytime soon. There is too much money to be made. In a lull in the almost ever-present self-enrichment process, a bunch of headless bodies—or just the heads—will be dropped somewhere conspicuous. And there may or may not be another note. Messages in Sinaloa no longer have to be written or explicit.

CHAPTER 1

IRAQ & THE AMERICAS:
3 GEN GANGS LESSONS AND PROSPECTS

Robert J. Bunker and John P. Sullivan
Initially published April 30, 2007

GANGS AND IRAQI INSURGENTS, militias, and other non-state groups share common origins based on tribalism, and therefore, it is expected that they will exhibit similar structures and behaviors. It is our belief that further insight into Iraq's present situation and future prospects may be derived from a perspective utilizing 3rd generation gang (3 GEN Gangs) studies which present lessons learned from the emergence and spread of gangs within the United States, and other parts of the world, over roughly the last four decades.[1] Basically, from a 3 GEN Gangs perspective, three generations of gangs have been found to exist: turf based, drug based, and mercenary based. The first generation gangs, comprising the vast majority, focus on protecting their turf. These gangs, the least developed of the three generational forms, provide both protection and identity to their members and little more. While some drug dealing is evident, it tends with these gangs to be a sideline activity.

The more evolved second and third generation gangs provide more tangible economic- and, later, political- based rewards to their members. Far fewer second generation gangs exist in relation to first generation gangs and, in turn, an even smaller number of third generation gangs exist in relation to second generation gangs—at least with regard to gangs found in the Americas. Second generation gangs focus on drug market development and exploitation and are far more sophisticated than turf based gangs. Third generation gangs are the most politicized, international in reach, and sophisticated of the gang generational forms. They will readily engage in mercenary endeavors and actively seek political power and financial gain from their activities. Certain terrorist groups (such as the Red Brigades in Italy), drug cartels, and local warlords all have attributes and organizational structures akin to third generation gangs.[2]

From a 3 GEN Gangs perspective, Iraq has been essentially overrun by 3rd generation gangs and their criminal-soldier equivalents. This is reminiscent of the nightmare scenario for the US already starting to develop in Central and South America (and, to a lesser extent, within the US) with the emergence, growth, and expansion of Mara Salvatrucha (MS-13) and other Maras. In many ways, the 'Gangs of Iraq' are a prelude to the 'Gangs of the Americas' that we will be increasingly facing in the Western Hemisphere.

Gangs emerge, prosper, and solidify their position as a viable social organizational form in housing projects, neighborhoods, prisons, slums, cities, urban regions, and even entire countries that have undergone (or are undergoing) varying forms of societal failure. The rise of newer forms of tribalism leading to gang emergence may be derived from combinations that include lack of jobs, high levels of poverty and drug abuse, low educational levels, an absence of functional families, along with high levels of crime and lawlessness, including that generated by domestic internal strife, which result in a daily threat of bodily injury. Further, newer forms of tribalism may readily mingle with older pre-existing forms of tribalism based on kinship, clan, and other extended family groupings.

Iraq's current situation, at least for the middle and southern sections, is far from hopeful. Currently some where between 1,000 and 5,000 people are now being killed throughout Iraq each month because of sectarian violence, gang wars, and rampant criminal activity. Total post-invasion deaths in Iraq taking place during the American and allied stability and support operations (SASO) period ranges anywhere from 50,000 to +100,000.[3] Societal strife generated by ethnic and religious intolerance— derived from older forms of Middle Eastern tribalism— has resulted in neighborhood ethnic cleansing and the emergence of fortified enclaves. Extra-judicial killings and torture (i.e. street justice) have become the norm as have home invasion robberies, carjackings, petty theft, assaults, and kidnappings for ransom. Shifting coalitions of former regime loyalists, foreign Jihadi fighters linked to al Qaeda, Shia and Sunni militiamen tied to local clerics, criminal gangs of numerous types, competing Iraqi ministries and even active military and police units, along with foreign operatives promoting the interests of Iran, Hizballah, and Syria make for a chaotic and ever-changing threat landscape.

Americans, once universally hailed as liberators except by the most hardened former regime loyalists, are now viewed by many Iraqis at best as unwanted foreigners that will hopefully leave soon and at worst as hated crusaders that should be actively singled out, tortured, and killed. The northern Kurd-dominated region of the country is far more stable and supportive of American forces than the two other sections of Iraq but still is not free of sectarian violence in the urban centers and sabotage, improvised explosive device (IED) attacks, suicide bombings, and assassinations occur throughout the region.

Insight can be gained by juxtaposing strife ridden Iraq with the US and other regions of the world, specifically Central and South America, with their high levels of gang emergence and activity. Gangs are very much a social cancer within American society and are a by-product of the new form of tribalism that has emerged nationally—possibly as a partial result of the demise of the older melting pot culture and an overemphasis on cultural relativism and heterogeneity.

As a consequence, gangs have spread at an alarming rate throughout American society. In the US, about 58 cities had gangs in 1960. By 1992, the number of cities with gangs had jumped to 769.[4] Luckily, the vast majority of gangs in the US are composed of the relatively less-evolved Turf gangs—though second generation drug gangs have been common for decades now and third generation mercenary gangs, in the current form of the Maras, have just recently started to appear within our borders.

Still, even though most gangs in the US are Turf-based gangs, gang-related homicides in our country have probably totaled about 100,000 over the last 20 years. This is an educated guess based on an extrapolation of Los Angeles county gang homicide data as no national gang homicide statistics exist.[5] The daily attrition rate on America's streets due to gang violence has either gone unrecognized or is not yet viewed as a national security threat by our federal government. To its credit, however, FBI led national task forces to contend with the criminal activities and atrocities (e.g. torture and machete attacks) committed by MS-13 and other violent gang members have now been put in place.[6]

In Central and South America, gangs are now nothing less than out of control. Honduras, El Salvador, Nicaragua, and Guatemala are all being directly threatened by the Maras.[7] In addition, Brazilian society was recently brought to its knees by a powerful prison gang that instigated a limited duration state wide insurgency that resulted in numerous civilian and law enforcement deaths and temporarily paralyzed the national economy.[8] Mexico, furthermore, is seeing a fusion of its powerful drug cartels and gangs with an ensuing drug war that is resulting in numerous killings and decapitations—much like the ritual Jihadi beheadings witnessed in Iraq.[9] No statistics or even estimates for the number of gang-related homicides that have taken place in Central and South America exist but they must surely be on par, if not far greater, than those that are estimated to have taken place in America over the last twenty years. If this is the case, gang killings for all of the Americas would now number, at the very least, in the low hundreds of thousands for that time span.

Of direct interest is the continuum of environmental modification represented by gang activities in the US at one extreme and in parts of the Americas and Iraq at the other. Even the most basic level US gangs will attempt to culturally influence and modify their surroundings with drive-by shootings, the use of gang graffiti to mark their territory, and the take over of selected public spaces. Iraqi gangs and groups, on the other hand, are engaging in full out ethnic cleansing, neighborhood takeovers, and direct political control of those individuals living within their sphere of influence. Early intervention can prevent gangs from taking over a neighborhood, city, urban region and other environments. However, if allowed to evolve and engage in unchecked activities for too long they promise to replace legitimate political authority. As such, 3 GEN Gangs readily fill the vacuum left by the absence of legitimate authority.

Iraq's future prospects, given this scenario are bleak. The domination of Iraq by 3 GEN Gangs and other non-state entities (e.g. insurgent and terrorist groups, the militias of the clerics, and renegade police, military, and private security forces) has destroyed any chance of a free and democratically unified country emerging anytime soon, or possibly even for decades to come. The Iraqi operational environment has now seen the total blurring of crime and war. Perhaps, it is now even too far gone to salvage from a traditional policing or military perspective—only time will tell in this regard.[10]

This brings us some measure of concern with regard to the future prospects vis-à-vis the gang situation in the Americas. As more and more 3 GEN Gangs begin to emerge, thrive, and expands their networks in the Western Hemisphere the long term prospects for large regions of the Americas may very well, at some point, also come into question. Currently, 3 GEN Gangs have already take control in slums and other urban no-go zones, prisons, and some provinces and territories of various states including Brazil, Colombia, Honduras, Nicaragua, El Salvador, Guatemala, and Mexico. That such gangs are now starting to emerge within the United States should also give pause for concern. These developments in global context may ultimately cause us to re-examine our policies in the Americas and elevate our concerns over the "Gangs of the Americas" to the same level as that currently afforded the "Gangs of Iraq."

CHAPTER 2

STATE OF SIEGE:
MEXICO'S CRIMINAL INSURGENCY

John P. Sullivan and Adam Elkus
Initially published August 19, 2008

MEXICO IS UNDER SIEGE, and the barbarians are dangerously close to breaching the castle walls. Responding to President Felipe Calderon's latest drug crackdown, an army of drug cartels has launched a vicious criminal insurgency against the Mexican state. So far, the conflict has killed over 1,400 Mexicans, 500 of them law enforcement officers.[1] No longer fearing retaliation, cartel gunmen assault soldier and high-ranking federale alike. The criminal threat is not only a threat to public order but to the state. A top-ranking Mexican intelligence official has noted in interview that criminal gangs pose a national security threat to the integrity of the state. Cartels are even trying to take over the Mexican Congress by funding political campaigns, CISEN director Guillero Valdes alleged.[2] Should Mexico's gangs cement their hold further, Mexico could possibly become a criminal-state largely controlled by narco-gangs. This is not just a threat to Mexico, however.

As the intensity of the violence grows, so does the possibility that Tijuana and Juarez's high-intensity street warfare will migrate north. Recent cartel warfare in Arizona indicates that America has become a battleground for drug cartels clashing over territory, putting American citizens and law enforcement at risk. But the northward migration of cartel warfare is not the worst consequence of Mexico's criminal insurgency. A lawless Mexico will be a perfect staging ground for terrorists seeking to operate in North America. American policymakers must act to protect our southern flank.

The Criminal State

Paradoxically, Mexico is a weak state troubled by a history of authoritarian domination. A deeply stratified nation with high unemployment, low real wages, systematic corruption, and extensive racial discrimination against its large Amerindian minority, Mexico has seen numerous revolutions and changes of government— often resulting in great bloodshed. Mexican historian Enrique Krauze argues that Mexico's current troubles stem from the rule of authoritarian strongmen.[3] Close to seventy years of one-party rule by the Institutional Revolutionary Party (PRI) and a socialist command economy have created a governmental culture of bribery, injustice, and impunity, particularly among internal security forces. Free trade, political reform, and the breaking of the PRI's oligarchic power have made Mexico more dynamic, but wealth and political power remain concentrated in the hands of a few.

Unfortunately, Mexico's corruption also has retarded the growth of its civil society. Without a strong and impartial law enforcement apparatus to protect them, journalists and honest civil servants have paid the ultimate price. 25 Mexican journalists have died under suspicious circumstances over the last 15 years,[4] and scores of judges, prosecutors, and politicians have been killed.[5] The culprits are depressingly familiar: cartel gunmen, rogue police, and other armed malcontents who see the free press and a strong judiciary as a threat to their interests.

Despite the centralization of political and economic power, the state is weak in Mexico's hinterlands, particularly the border regions. Corruption and the rise of criminal kingpins have feudalized Mexico, disrupting state power and the monopoly of force. As generations of American teenagers have discovered, the border regions in particular are temporary autonomous zones where one can do as he pleases without the threat of punishment. Border towns such a Tijuana are waypoints for massive amounts of commerce and contraband both supplied and demanded by globalization. While today's Mexico is not the veritable Wild West of Pancho Villa's time, there is an unmistakable continuity between the rule of the bandito and that of the cartel assassin. Command of the shadow economy guarantees riches and political influence.

One manifestation of the Mexican state's weakness is its burgeoning private security industry. At the turn of the millennium, Mexico's guns for hire contained an estimated 10,000 firms totaling at least 153,885 personnel, only 20% of which were registered. As in Russia, these private security forces have become private armies for the powerful, and implicated in the country's criminal violence. In some border regions of Mexico, private security firms decisively outnumber uniformed police officers and probably are better armed.[6]

Mexico's state weakness makes it an ideal transit point for drug smuggling into the United States. With enhanced security impeding the Florida drug smuggling route, 90% of cocaine sold in the United States passes through Mexico. Drug syndicates also supply the US market with ecstasy and methamphetamine.[7] However, Mexico also produces drugs of its own—in large quantities. In 2005, Mexico cultivated 3,300 hectares of opium poppy with a potential yield of 8 metric tons of pure heroin and 17 metric tons of "black tar" heroin. In the same year, drug producers also cultivated 5,600 hectares of marijuana with a potential production yield of 10,100 metric tons.[8] Many experts put drug profits at $40 billion, 20% of Mexican exports to the United States.[9]

Not surprisingly, the spoils of this massive underground economy are concentrated in the hands of a select few.[10] Mexico's drug trade can be categorized as "black globalization," a shadow economy that squashes legitimate enterprise, corrupts civil society, and fatally undermines the rule of law.[11] "Black globalization" also creates a neo-feudal power structure in which power flows to non-state forces controlling large slums. These fortresses of criminal influence are no-go areas for law enforcement and act as channeling points for the global illicit economy. Utilizing temporary autonomous zones in urban and rural centers, criminal can tap into a $2.5 trillion global illicit economy growing at 7 times the rate of growth in the legal economy.[12] This economy has created a massive criminal infrastructure to support it, with a complex network of sub-contracted specialists to handle virtually every task necessary to ensure that the clandestine goods reach their destination.[13] Needless to say, terrorists often exploit "black globalization" to create logistical networks and secure bases.

Coca Commanders

The Colombian Cali and Medellin cartels have traditionally dominated the drug economy in the Americas. However, their brazen challenges to state authority provoked the Colombian government's wrath. With the help of the United States, Colombian internal security forces successfully decapitated Cali and Medellin in the 1990s.[14] Hobbled by their brittle organizational structures, the Colombians could not regain their once fearsome power. But nature abhors a vacuum, and the Mexican cartels wasted no time in filling it.[15]

Seven Mexican cartels fight over the drug market. The Gulf, Sinaloa, and Juarez cartels are the largest. The Gulf cartel paired with the much smaller Tijuana cartel, and Juarez, Sinaloa, and Valencia have cooperated in the past.[16] However, alliances within the cartel system are constantly shifting and are based on convenience rather then personal or ideological ties. What was once an alliance today means nothing tomorrow, as each cartel's goal is to maximize its own advantage at the expense of its rivals. Any fixed taxonomy of alliances and networks should be viewed as suspect. So far, the latest round of murderous competition between the Gulf, Sinaloa, and resurgent Juarez cartels has killed over 4,000 Mexicans.[17]

Cartel managers don't do the dealing and killing themselves —they outsource to distributor gangs and freelance guns for hire called sicarios. While there are many gangs and subgangs carrying out this work, we will briefly look at how two such contractors— MS-13 and the Zetas—exemplify cartel operations.

MS-13 is a networked, "third generation" street gang operating in both the United States and Central America.[18] The product of unresolved turmoil from the Latin American civil wars of the 1980s, MS-13 commands 70,000 members south of the border.[19] The Maras are the Mexican cartels' retail salesmen, buying their methamphetamine and selling it in the United States.[20] Some have alleged that the cartels control MS-13, but the relationship between the two is purely business. MS-13 gets "street cred" and a potent product to sell, and the cartels get wide distribution.

Los Zetas are the elite soldiers of the drug war. One of many enforcer gangs servicing the cartels, the Zetas are a ruthless group of former Mexican special forces operators from the military and internal security services who sought a more financially rewarding profession. With their military expertise, the Gulf Cartel can carry out complex paramilitary operations against rivals and the Mexican government. The other cartels have developed their own enforcer gangs to counter the Zetas' Special Forces capabilities.

We largely supply the weapons. As many as 2,000 American weapons enter Mexico each day, helped by corrupt customs officials on both ends of the border.[21] The guns are smuggled by a swarm of "ant trails," small groups carrying one to two weapons each. Cartel arsenals brim with AK-47s, sniper scopes, grenade launchers, and "cop-killer" penetrative ammunition.[22] This firepower gives even the lowliest cartel gunman a tactical advantage over his police counterpart.

Worse yet, Mexico's cartels have surpassed their infamous Colombian antecedents. They have evolved into "Third-Phase Cartels," criminal-states that can pose a strategic threat to the nation-state.[23] Massive corruption has enabled the cartels to attach themselves to the Mexican state like parasites, slowly criminalizing it. Substantial chunks of Mexican infrastructure—police, judiciary, and public administration—are either weak or controlled by the cartels.[24] Police and local officials regularly protect cartel drug traffic and even carry out hits on behalf of cartel bosses.[25] As cartel influence grows within the government and Mexico's economy becomes more and more propped up by narcodollars, cartel co-option of the military becomes a frightening possibility. Perhaps this was why Mexican President Felipe Calderon decided to use force against the cartels, triggering the cartel campaign of terror.

Criminal Insurgency

In December 2006, Calderon launched a massive military offensive against the cartels, mobilizing 25,000 troops and federal police across the country.[26] This big push is not without precedent. Calderon's predecessor Vicente Fox had involved the military in counter-narcotics operations. But the scale, intensity, and commitment of Calderon's internal war dwarfs any of Fox's efforts. The Mexican government has opted for a blockhouse strategy, blanketing cartel-controlled territories with roadblocks and checkpoints to cut off cartel mobility and logistics. Military special operations units have targeted the Zetas and other enforcer gangs in sustained combat operations, raiding known cartel safe houses with overwhelming force.[27] Calderon has also expanded anti-corruption investigations to root our corrupt police.

The Mexican government's sustained intervention is designed to destroy the cartels and expand state authority. Unfortunately, Mexico's military approach lacks significant strategic communication operations, increased community policing, or public works investment—civil affairs tools that could build public confidence in the Mexican government's ability to curtail the cartels. Given the state of the public security forces and the corruption of the Mexican civil service, this may be an unfair criticism. Mexico may be incapable of mounting a broad-based civil affairs campaign and thus prioritizes hard power.

The ability of Mexico's military to tackle the cartels is also open to question. While Mexican military's counter-guerrilla capabilities have advanced in the wake of the 1994 Zapatista rebellion,[28] the cartels pose a different kind of threat. While the drug kingpins may not possess a force optimized for classical Maoist protracted warfare, they are deeply rooted within the basic infrastructure of the Mexican state. The military alone cannot root them out. In fact, utilization of the military for domestic law enforcement may backfire on the government, as human rights groups have not been shy in highlighting the numerous human rights abuses that the Mexican armed forces have been accused of the course of their counter-narcotics operations.[29] Additionally, the more the Mexican military involves itself in the drug war, the greater the chance that cartels will subvert and corrupt it.

Not surprisingly, the cartels have not sat idly by while Calderon cracks down. If the Mexican anti-crime effort succeeds, the state's powers will grow and the cartels will lose their influence—an unacceptable outcome to the narcos. In response, the cartels have launched a war of attrition against the government. The goal of this criminal insurgency is to roll back government power, preserve cartel assets, and teach Calderon and his successors a lesson: the cartel is king.

In describing cartel operations as a criminal insurgency, we do not suggest that the cartel structures are operating a unified operation against the Mexican state. Far from it—even the threat of a massive government crackdown is not enough to force the warring cartels to join forces. Rather the individual cartels are fighting each other and state forces to weaken the structures of governance and rule of law to secure maneuver room for their own operations and influence. We also do not mean to suggest that the goal of the criminal insurgent, like that of both classical and modern political insurgents—is the removal of foreign forces, the satisfaction of discrete political demands, or regime change.

The criminal insurgent is resolutely apolitical; he challenges the will of the state because he seeks to sever its regulatory arms. If the cartel insurgent has an ideal model of a Mexican state, it is a balkanized series of urban fiefs barely ruled by a supine national government that decides national and foreign policy. However, we use the term "insurgency" because it best describes the nature of the internal war waged by cartels against the Mexican state.

Cartel Strategy

Criminal insurgent strategy can be separated into three categories: attrition, psychological operations, and decapitation strikes. The criminal insurgents' long-term goal is to intimidate Mexico's government into quitting its anti-crime offensive. And if the federal government backs down after launching such a massive effort, public confidence and political will necessary for aggressive law enforcement will surely be lost. The target of the cartel's efforts is the whole of the Mexican government, beat cop to high-ranking civil servant.

Cartels are waging a war of attrition against low and middle-ranking Mexican law enforcement officers, the foot troops of the drug war. These operations consist of assassinations and small-unit ambushes. Police officers are frequently killed while off-duty, in transit, or operating in urban terrain. The vast majority of targets never have time to escape or return fire. Cartel gunmen, like most guerrillas, avoid stand-up confrontations with large formations of police or military forces. Truly amorphous, they form to strike when security officers are helpless and vulnerable. However, cartels operations have steadily grown more brazen. One recent raid aimed at destroying a fortified police command center.[30] Cartels have also utilized bombings, though to middling effect.[31]

Given the growth in cartel abilities, especially in complex operations, it is not unconceivable that cartel tactical abilities will continue to advance. Cartel gunmen already outmatch the tactical capabilities of most local Mexican police. The Brazilian First Capitol Command (PCC)'s 2006 urban terrorism campaign against São Paulo provides a model of how criminals may deploy swarming capabilities in urban battles against law enforcement. As John Robb notes, "gang members razed police stations, attacked banks, rioted in prisons, and torched dozens of buses, shutting down a transportation system serving 2.9 million people a day."[32] Brazilian public security officials were ruthlessly and systematically gunned down everywhere they could be found. Gang members killed police in their posts, neighborhood beats, and in their homes—while their families watched. The PCC operated in an emergent fashion, their violence organized by cell phone.[33]

Enforcer gangs such as the Zetas are the main element in cartel attrition operations, though local distributor gangs have also participated. These operations, however, would be impossible without the assistance of corrupt police and military officials.[34] Paid police assets and a network of spies provide cartels with intelligence on law enforce operations, allowing cartels to escape dragnets and gain the tactical advantage against police.[35] The cartels even succeeded in placing a spy in the President's office.[36]

Cartels followed up their murder campaigns with psychological operations urging police and the army to desert or become cartel gunmen. Recruiting banners are prominently displayed in Mexican cities, death lists are strewn throughout cemeteries, and police radios are hacked so cartels can personally deliver threats to officers.[37] Some police officers have even been beheaded, Al Qaeda-style.[38] These terror campaigns have taken their toll on police morale. Municipal police officers are increasingly asking themselves whether it is worth it to go up against the cartels—and their own corrupt colleagues. Entire small towns have seen their police forces quit, surrendering to the cartel onslaught.[39]

With the collusion of assets in high places, cartels have systematically targeted highranking Mexican criminal justice officials. Police chiefs, prosecutors, and judges are all wantonly targeted by cartel hitmen. In May, Edgar Millan Gomez and Robert Velasco Bravo, Mexico's two highest counter-narcotics officers, were shot dead.[40] In America, Gomez's rank was equivalent to head of the Federal Bureau of Investigation (FBI). The kills, as well as numerous disrupted paramilitary cells within Mexico City, show that the cartels are increasingly active in Mexico City and are capable of mounting operations against high-profile politicians.

Forward Defense In The Drug War

Mexico stands at a crossroads. A possibility exists that Mexico could very well become a criminal-state, with centralized criminal activity dominating the Mexican polity. Cartel power could become so deeply rooted within the Mexican state that uprooting it would mean civil war. Such an outcome would prove disastrous for American interests.

America bears a substantial interest in ensuring that our southern flank is stable and secure. That is why America has often intervened in Mexican affairs. France's 1860s attempt to colonize Mexico would have put a European imperial power on our border and had to be combated through military aid to Mexican insurgents and diplomatic pressure. Revolutionary instability in the early 1900s empowered Pancho Villa to strike across the border, provoking an American military mission deep into Mexican territory. In recent years, narcotics flows into the United States have fueled a domestic drug problem and empowered violent gangs on our streets. Instability and poverty in Mexico is also the cause of a massive wave of illegal immigration that shows no sign of abating.

A Mexican criminal-state would mean the spread of Mexico's violent cartel rivalries into American soil. America's already violent gang warfare could intensify as bigger powers enter the game. Already, as the Phoenix incident demonstrates, cartels are growing more brazen in their operations on American soil. A cartel hit team, disguised as a police tactical team, assassinated an American in Phoenix, Arizona. The cartel gunmen almost killed a police SWAT team that responded on the scene.[41] This has not been the only case—cartel hit teams have been reported operating in other border regions. Mexican kidnapping gangs have already been reported operating against American citizens.[42] Additionally, the vast monetary power of the cartels could subvert low-level civil government and politics within border regions.

Worst of all, a failed state situation within Mexico would provide an ample staging area for terrorists seeking to operate in the Americas. It is in America's national interest to ensure that Mexico does not become a large version of Ciudad del Este in the South American tri-border region, where all manner of criminals and terrorists have taken up residence. Mexican gangs already smuggle hundreds of thousands of foreigners across the border, there is an increasing likelihood that some of them will be terrorists.

Some may be tempted to close off the border with soldiers, thinking the problem can be walled off. This is no solution. Closure of the border's lucrative trade routes would devastate both American and Mexican economies. Furthermore, firewalling porous borders from the entry of decentralized non-state groups is not a safe proposition in today's globalized world. Men, material, and capital move freely, regardless of outmoded views of national sovereignty. America must take the offensive to prevent Mexico from falling to the cartels.

The root of the problem is American demand for Mexican-supplied drugs. Barring a large-scale policy shift, this problem is not likely to change. Expanded efforts to cut demand and increase interdiction efficiency may be of small importance, and the US must certainly cut off the flow of illicit arms to Mexico can help, as American firepower is currently killing hundreds of Mexican policemen and soldiers. But with the wealth and resources of cartels, they can easily procure other weapons, although at a much greater cost. That being said, doing so will be a measure of good faith to Mexicans increasingly suspicious of the US's level of commitment in the drug war.

The only real long-term solution is a sustained intervention in Mexico's drug war approaching the scale and resources of Plan Colombia. The Merida Initiative, a recently approved $400 million aid package, is a step in the right direction. Vermont Senator Patrick Leahy, the bill's author, has emphasized that the bill is not a blank check, and will be provided only when Mexico demonstrates compliance with transparency, human rights, and accountability standards. However, concerns have been raised about the bill's lack of coverage in crucial areas of prevention and rehabilitation, or crop conversion. Additionally, it is yet to be seen whether Mexico's famously corrupt security forces will swallow up the money.[43]

Unlike Plan Colombia, which focused on building up military counternarcotics efforts, America's intervention should focus on building up Mexico's law enforcement and internal security forces. American law enforcement agencies should intensify intelligence cooperation with their Mexican counterparts. Loose cooperation already exists between Mexican and American law enforcement agencies, but this cooperation must be institutionalized for it to have any real effect. American Special Forces and intelligence assets could also be deployed to garner signals intelligence—a precedent exists in the Intelligence Support Activity's use of signal intelligence assets to track down Pablo Escobar in Colombia.[44] Expanded cooperation on both sides of the border is necessary, as cartel operations are truly a hemispheric problem. America enjoys an advantage in its relative security and law enforcement control—thus important Mexican witnesses can be protected in the United States and more aggressive American operations can be mounted stateside against cartel operatives. Military advisers and expeditionary police units can also play a role in helping build Mexican forces. Mexican police already receive limited training from American advisors, but an expanded advisor corps of American police could do much to bring up the quality of Mexico's lawmen. Raising the salaries of Mexican municipal police may also help make them more resistant to corruption.

However, American assistance will be most valuable in helping to build up Mexican civil society. Only through a careful reconstruction of the rule of law can the cartels power ultimately be dialed back to manageable level. Law enforcement and military aid can only go so far in dealing with far rooted problems of authority, accountability, and infrastructure. This will be a delicate process—the United States cannot push too hard, as Mexico (nor any other nation) does not take kindly to lectures about human rights and transparency.

Policing and law enforcement services are essential to community stability, stable governance and effective functioning of the rule of law. Many parts of Mexico have become areas of "limited statehood." These "criminal enclaves" have become de facto "Lawless zones" where the barbarization of crime and conflict dominate.[45] Maintaining or revitalizing stability and order in Mexico must become the priority of both Mexico and the United States. This will require action on both sides of the border.

Community policing and intelligence-led policing strategies can help at the tactical and operational levels. New levels of community trust need to be built in Mexican villages, cities, and states. This will require a high degree of local, state, federal and cross-border cooperation. Multilateral coordination, intelligence-sharing and enforcement efforts must be bolstered. This will require a concerted effort to eliminate corruption and build skills and professional trust needed for effective cross-border interaction.

In addition to Federal programs, in both the United States of America and Mexico, crossborder programs involving the four US and ten Mexican "Border States"[46] will be needed. Personnel exchanges, joint-training, and skill-building among police, intelligence and judicial officials could help build the required skill-base and knowledge needed to revitalize and sustain the stability needed for countering cartels. The Border Governors Conference/Conferencia de Gobernadores Fronterizos is an ideal forum for starting this cross-border security cooperation. Comprised of the governors and their staffs from all ten "border states," it meets annually and conducts on-going coordination through a series of worktables, including border security.

Neither Mexico nor the United States can eliminate drug trafficking, but what it can do is shrink the cartels into more manageable, localized entities unable to pose a threat to the Mexican state. Such a task is daunting, and may strike most as impossible. But the example of Italy is instructive—the Sicilian mafia once routinely assassinated mayors and judges that it did not like. But a team of American-Italian law enforcement gumshoes pounding pavement on both sides of the Atlantic amassed enough evidence to cut the mafia down to size.[47] Perhaps in a generation or so, Mexican gangbangers will be less Al Capone and more Snoop Dogg—old, posturing, and irrelevant.

CHAPTER 3

PLAZAS FOR PROFIT:
MEXICO'S CRIMINAL INSURGENCY

John P. Sullivan and Adam Elkus
Initially published April 26, 2009

IN AUGUST 2008, WE published an essay in *Small Wars Journal* called "State of Siege: Mexico's Criminal Insurgency."[1] We were concerned at the lack of attention and policy discussion paid to the growing cartel violence in Mexico, which we called a "criminal insurgency." Now it is hard to escape discussion of Mexico's drug war. While we are heartened that security commentators are now focusing on Mexico, we feel that the "failed state" debate is at best a distraction that diverts discussion of the issue and a concrete discussion of the conflict's political-military dynamics would be more productive. We have updated our earlier assessment to include new events and trends in Mexico's criminal insurgency, and we will continue to periodically revise our assessment as the dynamics of the conflict evolve.

In broad scope, US policy should focus on helping Mexico rebuild the rule of law while hedging against cartel actions on the border. To do so, the US must engage both informal Mexican governing networks and help construct new cross-border partnerships that can act as policy shops for coordinating policy response and military/law enforcement cooperation against the cartels. At the same time, revamping of domestic security approaches also are needed to guard against overflow of drug war violence.

Overview: Criminal Insurgency and the Plazas

The first precondition of victory in war is to understand what kind of war you are fighting. Mexico is currently wracked by *criminal insurgency*, a frequently misunderstood form of political violence. As Army War College professor Steven Metz notes in his Strategic Studies Institute (SSI) monograph *Rethinking Insurgency*, not all insurgencies conform to the classic Leninist or Maoist models. Some insurgents don't want to take over the government or force it to accede to ideological demands. They want a piece of the state that they can use to develop parallel structures for profit. Inasmuch as they use political violence to accomplish this instrumental goal, they are insurgents— albeit of a criminal variety.[2]

Subversion, infiltration and general capture of governmental, corporate, and societal organs by non-state actors are also strong elements of criminal insurgency. Criminal insurgents' goals are to capture public goods and divert them to their own ends. The purpose of criminal violence within this framework is to overcome state resistance to this subversion of sovereignty and fight off competing claims to public goods by sub and supra-state actors and corrupted state elites. Analysts used to thinking about insurgency through strictly ideological, religious, or classical Maoist models often mistake criminal insurgency for ordinary drug violence, misunderstanding the danger inherent in Mexico's criminal insurgency. The contested spaces that these criminal insurgents are fighting over are the "plazas"— the corridors for shipment of drugs into the United States. It is clear that the plazas are the vital terrain of the criminal insurgency— and may even constitute certain cartels' centers of gravity. There is also an increasingly regional dimension to this struggle. As STRATFOR analyst Stephen Meiners writes, increased drug trafficking along Central American land routes is widening the operational space into many Central American nations— most of which are even more unprepared than Mexico to handle the surge of crime.[3]

Is Mexico a failed state? This question should be regarded as a distraction. Absent a few egregious cases such as Somalia, most states usually do not "fail." Rather, states that experience a prolonged shift in their internal dynamics *change* to different forms of sovereignty. While certain forms of sovereignty may be preferable to others, state change is not equivalent to state failure. The heated debate over whether or not

Mexico is a failed state obscures the operational and strategic dynamics of the criminal insurgency and possible policy solutions.

Operational Dynamics of Criminal Insurgency

Since 2007, Mexican President Felipe Calderon has deployed the military against the cartels. His strategy consists of direct action raids by general-purpose forces and special operations forces as well as clampdown in many regions where cartel action is strong. At present, around 40,000 Mexican soldiers are engaged in the drug war.[4] Troops have also been placed in civil law enforcement command roles.[5]

The use of Mexico's military, known in the past for human rights violations, has alienated some civilians and worried human rights groups.[6] Military force also triggered a bloody eruption of retaliatory cartel violence. Attacks on civilians, decapitations, and other horrific acts of violence are commonplace. The military itself has been targeted for cartel penetration and brutalization. As the main effort against the cartels, the military is the only force that can match cartel firepower and tactical cohesion—and thus a prime target for cartel enforcers. Mexican area specialist George W. Grayson, a professor at the College of William and Mary, recounts one particularly brutal incident involving the cartel enforcer gang Los Zetas:

> "In December 2008, Los Zetas captured and executed eight Army officers and enlisted men in Guerrero, a violence-torn, impoverished southern state where a "dual sovereignty" exists between the elected government and narco-criminals. Pictures of the decapitated cadavers lying side-by-side flashed around the world on television and YouTube. In February 2009, the paramilitaries killed retired Brigadier General Mauro Enrique Tello Quinones. They broke his arms and legs before driving him into the jungle and executing him; his corpse and those of two aides were discovered two days after the mayor of Cancun hired Tello Quinones to form a SWAT team to fight such criminals."[7]

These gruesome displays, along with less violent psychological operations, have had a negative effect on military morale. Mexican defense officials estimate that 100,000 soldiers have quit to join the cartels over the last seven years.[8] Cartels have also directed psychological operations utilizing paid front groups to foment anti-military protests, buying off poor Mexicans and putting them in the streets to protest against the government response.[9] However, some opposition is motivated by legitimate grievances over the harshness and bluntness of the overwhelmingly enemy-centric military response.

Adding to the problem are constitutional limits placed on military forces operating against cartels. Soldiers are barred from performing many aspects of basic police work and can only detain individuals they catch in the commission of the crime. They also must obtain search warrants from police, who often tip off cartels before soldiers can arrest them. These civil-military restraints motivate military law breaking, as soldiers see no other way to accomplish their objectives.[10]

As Grayson rightfully notes, the weakness of Mexico's civilian law enforcement and judicial institutions make reliance on the military unavoidable. Cartels easily outgun most Mexican police on the municipal level, many of whom elect to flee rather than fight a battle that they cannot possibly win. To make matters worse, Mexico's National Audit Office concluded that a staggering 50 percent of municipal police officers were unfit for service.[11] In light of this data, Calderón's goal of replacing the military with civilian law enforcement by the end of his term in 2012 is overly optimistic.

Increased American border policing, supply-side crackdowns, and intelligence cooperation have also augmented the Mexican military surge. US arrests have put hundreds of American-based cartel members in jail. Law enforcement agencies have also cracked down on illegal gun transfers, a major source of weaponry for cartels. Thus far, the Obama administration has allocated $700 million for a border surge against the cartels.[12] A higher level of cooperation and intensive coordination are necessary to build upon this initial investment. How do we measure the effectiveness of the combined Mexican-American effort? The Mexican government can certainly boast impressive metrics: 60,000 arrested, 32,000 weapons and 4 million bullets, $320 million in cash, seventy tons of cocaine, and 4,000 tons of marijuana seized.[13] This is a qualitative improvement over past numbers. But Mexico still manages to supply roughly 90% of America's cocaine, and drug profits remain high at roughly $60 billion a year.[14] Keep in mind however, that a lack of precise figures means that this number could easily be inaccurate, as other estimates have put the drug metrics at $10 billion.[15] The criminal insurgency has claimed 6,000 dead in 2008 and at least 1,600 dead since the beginning of this year.[16] The Mexican government also claims that sustained pressure on the cartels has lowered the supply of cocaine, raised its price, and diminished its purity. News reports also indicate that Europe may be eclipsing the United States, as demand for cocaine at twice the price has positioned the Colombians to once again become a prime supplier.[17]

The problem with arrest and seizure metrics is that they conflate the ebb and flow of the drug war—which may never end—with the specific issue of the criminal insurgency. Cartel goals have evolved over time to the exercising of "dual sovereignty" over the "plazas" and the purpose of the Mexican government crackdown is to erase that sovereignty. Are the cartels succeeding? If we define the minimum cartel objective as preserving their sovereign autonomy and surviving the government assault, the answer is yes. Sovereignty in Mexico is at times "stratified" as cartels continue to exercise control over numerous contested zones within enclaves of the Mexican state.

The cartels are also engaged in a fierce internal competition over drug transportation routes, the ferocity of which rivals the nominal war with the Mexican government. In fact, most of the drug war dead are casualties of this internal cartel war. It is a testament to the fragility of Mexican law enforcement institutions that Mexican cartels are able to wage war against each other and against the Mexican government at the same time.

Particularly worrying are several changes in cartel operational dynamics since our initial paper. First, there is the prospect of a truce between the two largest cartels—the Gulf and Federation groups. Some open-source news reports reference ongoing negotiations between the two to pool their resources against both their competitors and the government. If these news reports are indeed accurate, this truce would build a combined force of approximately 100,000 cartel enforcers.[18] However, precise information on the size, strength, training standards, and armaments of cartels is hard to find and alliances between cartels and their gang partners shift regularly.

Cartel enforcer gangs are also on the rise as independent organizations. Cartels traditionally have a fluid and complicated relationship with their hired guns, but enforcer gangs are growing fat off their drug profits. They are using these gains to enlarge their organizations into larger networked assemblages. As Sam Logan notes, the most violent enforcer gang, Los Zetas, is morphing into a "Zeta

Organization" that acts apart from their traditional overlords in the Gulf Cartel.[19] Zeta's transition is troubling, since it is one of the most well-armed and lethal enforcer gangs. However, the Zeta advantage is relative as many cartels are steadily increasing their armaments and upgrading their tactical skills.

Los Angeles Times reporters Ken Ellingwood and Tracy Wilkinson report that "Traffickers have escalated their arms race, acquiring military-grade weapons, including hand grenades, grenade launchers, armor-piercing munitions and antitank rockets with firepower far beyond the assault rifles and pistols that have dominated their arsenals."[20] These weapons include .50 caliber Barrett sniper rifles, M203 40-millimeter grenade launchers, light anti-tank weapons (LAWs), and possibly even improvised explosive devices (IEDs).[21] The new cartel weapons Ellingwood and Wilkinson report go far beyond the usual cartel armaments, and demonstrate that smuggled American guns are only a part of the problem.

Cartels are also learning and practicing traditional squad infantry tactical concepts and engaging in pitched gun battles with Mexican army patrols.[22] Greater cohesion and improved weaponry allows them to mix and match their usual mixture of assassination tactics and a limited form of positional engagement. However, their overall techniques, tactics, and procedures remain the same: attack the government and then melt away. And as military personnel continue to desert and join the cartels, drug gangs' tactical acumen will continue to increase.

Another troubling trend is criminal insurgent radicalization of vulnerable youth on both sides of the border. Radicalization is not something that happens solely in religious or ideological insurgency, and the same dynamics of radicalization observed in Marc Sageman's pioneering studies are present in street gangs and cartel enforcer units. The good drug gangs provide is a sense of purpose, belonging, and even a quasi-supernatural sensation of invincibility and righteousness—very much like the "bunches of guys" Sageman observes amid diasporas in Europe. Criminal insurgent radicalization can be observed in the cult of personality venerating La Santa Muerte (also known as Santisma Muerte), the death saint.[23] Hitmen offer toasts to the death saint with the blood of their enemies, reveling in feelings of invincibility and power.[24]

Corrections officials have observed that many inmates are increasingly found with Santa Muerte paraphernalia. Portraits of the death saint have also been found in many drug labs.[25] Cartels fund many shrines to the death saint in Mexico and use it as a symbol of their power, and Mexican officials have destroyed statues and shrines to Santisma Muerte in cartel-dominated border cities.[26] This is unfortunate, as Santa Muerte, despite her grim appearance, is one of Mexico's many folk saints. The hijacking of this otherwise benign religious symbol to use as a tool of cartel radicalization is reminiscent of the usage of folk saints as symbols of war in Africa's many irregular conflicts. An equally insidious development is the recruiting of child assassins and other young men as hitmen for cartel-affiliated drug gangs on both sides of the border. Cartels and drug gangs are increasingly recruiting "sicaritos," young teens and pre-teens whose youthful bravado and desire to prove their manhood make them excellent cannon fodder.[27] Again, there is a gruesome parallel to the usage of child soldiers both inside and outside of the Americas and negative implications for the chances of reintegration of these sicaritos back into society.[28]

Strategic Dynamics of Criminal Insurgency

In order to better understand the strategic dynamics of Mexico's criminal insurgency, we suggest considering the framework of the parallel state. As the Spanish think-tank FRIDE notes, the term "parallel state" is increasingly used in political science circles to describe "the existence of a clandestine nexus between formal political leadership, self-serving factions within the state apparatus, organized crime and/or experts in violence."[29] Parallel states often include deeply embedded networks of negative actors who exert power through both covert influence and armed violence. These actors distort official state policy to protect their interests, a dynamic that American and Afghani security chiefs are well aware of in Pakistan. Public goods are diverted towards these actors, making the fulfillment of various state obligations problematic even as the appearance of a legitimate public sector is maintained. A parallel state also involves parallel modes of sovereignty, with multiple competitors to state power existing within a neo-feudal patchwork of the ostensibly solid state.

The problem of cartels is essentially the problem of multiple "parallel states." All of the functions of legitimate and sovereign government continue, but substantial public goods are diverted to benefit non-state networks. A criminal-gang nexus has burrowed like a malignant parasite into the superstructure of the state. And for a while, it was progressively tolerated as long as it did not cause trouble for the Mexican state. But obviously with the election of Calderón this implicit understanding could no longer be maintained. The cartel aim is to restore the status quo ante and as long as this goal remains limited it has a high chance of success. Should cartels overreach—and there are signs that they may be doing so—they will probably cause their own destruction. The example of Colombia is illustrative. Pablo Escobar's campaign of terror challenged government control so much that the Colombian government backed a militia called "Los Pepes" that effectively decapitated the cartel leadership.

What is the future of Mexico's criminal insurgency? More worrying than an unlikely systemic collapse is the slow infection of cartel parallel structures into the superstructure of the Mexican state. As the violent struggle to control the plazas escalates, parallel state embeds itself within deeper and deeper within each contested zone. Success against the cartels is not out of the pale, but uprooting the deep state network that protects the parallel state does not seem likely at this juncture. Further criminalization and the growth of hollow zones are increasingly likely given present trends. Continued military involvement risks increasing corruption of rank-and-file soldiers and the growth of cartel combat power.

What is the nature of the danger to the United States? Now that American federal law enforcement is positioning for border force stabilization missions, we are increasingly thrusting ourselves into the battle for the "plazas." Will the cartels respond by targeting law enforcement officers and civil servants? It's hard to tell, as by doing so cartels would bring down the full wrath of the American law enforcement and military on their shoulders. So far, violence in crossborder incursions has mainly targeted civilians involved in the drug trade, although law enforcement officers have been attacked in several incidents, the most famous being the 22nd of June hit in Phoenix, Arizona.[30] We see little evidence to believe that cartels have a strategic plan in place to attack law enforcement officials. This may change, however, if cartel power grows or cartels perceive that they can similarly bleed American will at an acceptable cost. Law enforcement intelligence must closely monitor cartel and gang activity to discern their plans and force structure.

The strategic problem of a contested zone on the border also cannot be overlooked. Besides the obvious risk of cross-border infiltration by foreign powers, booming cross-border trade could be imperiled by a fundamentally hollow, lawless, and violent border. The growth of cartel power, the intensity of the growing warfare, and the increasingly transnational context of gang crime signify that Mexico's criminal insurgency is likely to have ripple effects north of the border.

Recommendations

On the purely domestic and tactical level, police must prepare for cartel warfare. Lessons from the Mexican drug war should be incorporated into training scenarios and wargames. Police must be prepared to engage opponents much more heavily armed and operationally adept than the average gangbanger. This does not solely mean beefing up police with advanced weaponry— rather, they must be empowered to perform "full-spectrum policing." Full spectrum policing covers the range of public order functions ranging from everyday community policing, through gang suppression to counterterrorism and counterinsurgency. Police must be able to carry out these missions without sacrificing their relationship to the communities they protect. This is a doctrinal, organizational, and training issue that we have explored in our paper "Postcard from Mumbai: Modern Urban Siege."[31]

Intelligence and analysis resources must also be devoted to geosocial red-team analysis of cartel aims, structures, and activities in order to develop better information for tactical, operational, and strategic decision-making. Counterinsurgency principles should be carefully blended with traditional community policing and beat management techniques to prevent the growth of parallel cartel-governance structures, deter the smuggling of weaponry across the border, and develop intelligence that can inform strategic decision-making about cartel links to evolving enforcer gangs. Firewalling off the problem behind a giant fence is most emphatically not an option. Many of the cartels, and their affiliated gangs, have large operations well beyond the border regions— Mexican cartels spar with local gangs as far north as Canada.[32] On the domestic grand strategic level, a review of drug war strategy should be conducted. Drug policy shifts, however, are unlikely in the short-term, so police, military, and intelligence agencies must work with the policy tools available.

Foreign cooperation and resources with Mexico must be intensified, especially in advisory training of police and military. However, the bulk of this assistance must go towards building up the capabilities of police and helping Mexico root out corruption, rebuild the rule of law, and sustain robust community institutions. It is important to note, that the most promising outcome of the recent cross-border dialogue about the drug wars is an awareness of the need to accept "coresponsibility" for solving the threat. Crucial to this task is the development of network structures. Mexico area expert and network warfare theorist David Ronfeldt, writing in his blog *Apropos of Two Theories*, is emphatic on this point. Both Mexico's informal camarilla elite cliques and the new political structures built since the decline of PRI power are crucial to beating back the cartels. And, as Ronfeldt notes, they also mesh with the emerging military/intelligence, and law enforcement partnerships being constructed on both sides of the Rio Grande.[33]

It takes a network to fight a network, and building a genuine Mexican-American networked force structure for counter-netwar requires the construction and strengthening of both formal and informal Mexican-American security networks, partnerships, working groups, and other such structures. There is a risk of cartel infiltration but sound vetting and operational security measures can minimize this danger. The US should do its best to help shape the conditions that enable our southern neighbor to succeed fighting its battle with the brigands. The strategic aim for US-Mexican cooperation should be to minimize cartel activity to a level that does not threaten legitimate government functioning (and effective control) at all levels of governance— federal, state, and municipal. The larger issues of changing state dynamics, as embodied by parallel states, are not going to go away nor are they easily resolvable by the US. Nevertheless, we can reduce the risk to ourselves and help Mexico contain its cartels, and collectively, limit the potential for criminal insurgency throughout the Western hemisphere.

CHAPTER 4

FUTURE CONFLICT: CRIMINAL INSURGENCIES, GANGS AND INTELLIGENCE

John P. Sullivan
Initially published May 31, 2009

GANGS DOMINATE THE INTERSECTION between crime and war. Traditionally viewed as criminal enterprises of varying degrees of sophistication and reach, some gangs have evolved into potentially more dangerous and destabilizing actors. In many areas across the world—especially in 'criminal enclaves' or 'lawless zones' where civil governance, traditional security structures, and community or social bonds have eroded—gangs thrive. This essay[1] briefly examines the dynamics of crime and war in these contested regions. Specifically, it provides a framework for understanding 'criminal insurgencies' where acute and endemic crime and gang violence challenge the solvency of state political control.

Criminal gangs come in many forms. They challenge the rule of law and employ violence to dominate local communities. In some cases they are expanding their reach and morphing into a new warmaking entities capable of challenging the legitimacy and even the solvency of nation-states. This potential brings life to the prediction made by Martin van Creveld who noted, "In the future, war will not be waged by armies but by groups whom today we call terrorists, guerrillas, bandits and robbers, but who will undoubtedly hit upon more formal titles to describe themselves."[2]

Some advanced gangs—known as 'third generation gangs' and/ or maras—are waging 'wars" and changing the dynamics of crime. In some extreme cases they are waging a de facto criminal insurgency. As Adam Elkus and I recently noted: "Criminal insurgency is haunting the police stations and barracks of North America. Powerful criminal networks increasingly challenge the state's monopoly on force, creating new threats to national security."[3] Mexico is currently challenged by extreme criminal violence,[4] but it is by no means the only state in the Americas suffering from criminal insurgency. Transnational criminal organizations ranging from the transnational street collective Mara Salvatrucha (MS-13) to the powerful Mexican drug cartels are steadily increasing in both power and reach. Even some American street gangs are evolving into 'third generation' gangs: large, networked, transnational bodies that may yet develop true political consciousness.[5]

Criminal insurgency presents a challenge to national security analysts used to creating simulations and analytical models for terrorism and conventional military operations. Criminal insurgency is different from "regular" terrorism and insurgency because the criminal insurgents' sole political motive is to gain autonomy economic control over territory. They do so by hollowing out the state and creating criminal enclaves to maneuver.[6]

Global Gangs/Transnational Crime

These criminal gangs and their impact is no longer a localized criminal issue. Transnational gangs and crime have hemispheric and global potentials. Gangs are essentially a form of organized crime and in an age of globalization, transnational or global crime can change the nature of war and politics.

These potentials find their underpinnings in the virulence of transnational crime. Transnational crime has effectively become a threat to political, economic, environmental and social systems worldwide. This threat involves more than drug trafficking. In addition to the substantial illegal global drug trade and its attendant violence, transnational crime also embraces major fraud, corruption and manipulation of both political and financial systems. Canadian intelligence analyst Samuel Porteous describes this, explaining that transnational crime undermines civil society, political systems and state sovereignty by normalizing violence and legitimizing corruption. It also erodes society by distorting market mechanisms through the disruption of equitable commercial transactions, and degrades the environment by sidelining environmental regulation and safeguards. All these potentials have the cumulative effect of destabilizing nations and economies.[7]

Transnational gangs and criminals extend their reach and influence by co-opting individuals and organizations through bribery, coercion and intimidation to "facilitate, enhance, or protect"[8] their activities. As a consequence, these groups are emerging as a serious impediment to democratic governance and a free market economy. This danger is particularly evident in Mexico, Colombia, Nigeria, Russia and other parts of the Former Soviet Union where corruption has become particularly insidious and pervasive. At sub-national levels, such corruption can also have profound effects. At a neighborhood level, political and operational corruption can diminish public safety, placing residents at risk to endemic violence and inter-gang conflict, essentially resulting in a "failed community." This is the virtual analog of a "failed state."[9]

Examining Cartel Evolution

Drug cartels are one type of organized criminal enterprise that have challenged states and created "lawless zones" or criminal enclaves. Examining cartel evolution can help illuminate the challenges to states and civil governance posed by criminal gangs and cartels. Robert J. Bunker and I looked at cartel evolution and related destabilizing potentials in our 1998 paper "Cartel Evolution: Potentials and Consequences."[10] In that paper, we identified three potential evolutionary phases. These are described below.

1st Phase Cartel (Aggressive Competitor)

The first phase cartel form originated in Colombia during the 1980s and arose as an outcome of increasing US cocaine demand. This type of cartel, characterized by the Medellín model, realized economies of scale not known to the individual cocaine entrepreneurs of the mid-1970s. This early cartel was an aggressive competitor to the Westphalian state because of its propensity for extreme violence and willingness to directly challenge the authority of the state.

2nd Phase Cartel (Subtle Co-Opter)

The second phase cartel form also originally developed in Colombia, but in this instance, is centered in the city of Cali. Unlike their Medellín counterparts, the Cali cartel was shadowy organization devoid of an actual kingpin. Its organization is more distributed and network-like, rather than hierarchical. Many of its characteristics and activities were stealth-masked and dispersed, which yielded many operational capabilities not possessed by the first phase cartel form. Specifically, it possessed leadership clusters that are more difficult to identify and target with a decapitation attack. The Cali cartel was also more sophisticated in its criminal pursuits and far more likely to rely upon corruption, rather than violence or overt political gambits, to achieve its organizational ends. This cartel form has also spread to Mexico with the rise of the Mexican Federation, an alliance of the "big four" mafias based in Tijuana, Sonora, Juárez, and the Gulf. This dynamic is still evolving.

3rd Phase Cartel (Criminal State Successor)

Third Phase Cartels, if and when they emerge, have the potential to pose a significant challenge to the modern nation-state and its institutions. A Third Phase Cartel is a consequence of unremitting corruption and co-option of state institutions. While this "criminal state successor" has yet to emerge, warning signs of its eventual arrival are present in many states worldwide. Of current importance in the United States are the conditions favoring narco- or criminal-state evolution in Mexico. Indeed, the criminal insurgency in Mexico could prove to be the genesis of a true third phase cartel, as Mexican cartels battle among themselves and the state for dominance. Essentially, third phase cartels rule criminal enclaves, acting much like warlords.

Criminal Enclaves

The fullest development of a criminal enclave exists in the South American jungle at the intersection of three nations. Ciudad del Este, Paraguay is the center of this criminal near free state. Paraguay, Brazil and Argentina converge at this riverfront outpost. A jungle hub for the world's outlaws, a global village of outlaws, the triple border zone serves as a free enclave for significant criminal activity, including people who are dedicated to supporting and sustaining acts of terrorism. Denizens of the enclave include Lebanese gangsters and terrorists, drug smugglers, Nigerian gangsters and Asian mafias: Japanese Yakuza, Tai Chen (Cantonese mafia), Fuk Ching, the Big Circle Boys, and the Flying Dragons. This polyglot mix of thugs demonstrates the potential of criminal netwarriors to exploit the globalization of organized crime.[11]

The blurring of borders— a symbol of the post-modern, information age— is clearly demonstrated here, where the mafias exploit interconnected economies. With the ability to overwhelm governments weakened by corruption and jurisdictional obstacles, the mafias of Ciudad del Este and its Brazilian twin city of Foz do Iguacu demonstrate remarkable power and reach. Terrorism interlocks with organized crime in the enclave, a post-modern free city that is a haven to Middle Eastern terrorists, a hub for the global drug trade, a center consumer product piracy, and base for gunrunners diverting small arms (form the US) to the violent and heavily armed drug gangs in the favelas of Rio de Janeiro and São Paulo.

The convergence of cartel evolution and manifestation of inter-netted criminal enterprises is so pronounced in this enclave, Robert Bunker and I call this the third phase cartel the Ciudad del Este model.[12] The transnational criminal organizations here demonstrate the potential for criminal networks to challenge state sovereignty and gain local dominance. These networked "enclaves" or a third phase cartel embracing similar characteristics could become a dominant actor within a network of transnational criminal organizations, and potentially gain legitimacy or at least political influence within the network of state actors. Mexico's current battle for the 'plazas' may be an early manifestation of criminal enclave formation.

Transnational Gangs

Transnational gangs are another state challenger. They are a concern throughout the Western Hemisphere. Criminal street gangs have evolved to pose significant security and public safety threats in individual neighborhoods, metropolitan areas, nations, and across borders. Such gangs—widely known as maras— are no longer just street gangs. They have morphed across three generations through interactions with other gangs and transnational organized crime organizations (e.g., narcotics cartels/drug trafficking organizations) into complex networked threats.[13]

Transnational maras have evolved into a transnational security concern throughout North and Central America. As a result of globalization, the influence of information and communications technology, and travel/migration patterns, gangs formerly confined to local neighborhoods have spread their reach across neighborhoods, cities and countries. In some cases, this reach is increasingly cross-border and transnational. Current transnational gang activity is a concern in several Central American States and Mexico (where they inter-operate with cartels).[14]

Transnational gangs can be defined as having one or more of the following characteristics: 1) criminally active and operational in more than one country; 2) criminal operations committed by gangsters in one country are planned, directed, and controlled by leadership in another country; 3) they are mobile and adapt to new areas of operations; and 4) their activities are sophisticated and transcend borders.[15] The gangs most frequently mentioned in this context are Mara Salvatrucha (MS-13) and Eighteenth Street (M-18), both originating in the barrios of Los Angeles. In order to understand the potential reach and consequences of transnational maras it is useful to review third generation gang theory.

Street Gangs: Three Generations on the Road to Netwar

A close analysis of urban and transnational street gangs shows that some of these criminal enterprises have evolved through three generations—transitioning from traditional turf gangs, to market-oriented drug gangs, to a new generation that mixes political and mercenary elements. The organizational framework for understanding contemporary gang evolution was first explored in a series of papers starting with the 1997 article "Third Generation Street Gangs: Turf, Cartels, and Netwarriors." These concepts were expanded in another article with the same title, and the model further refined in the 2000 *Small Wars and Insurgencies* paper "Urban Gangs Evolving as Criminal Netwar Actors."[17] In these papers (and others), I observed that gangs could progress through three generations. As gangs negotiate this generational shift, their voyage is influenced by three factors: politicization, internationalization, and sophistication. This gang form the 'third generation' gang entails many of the organizational and operational attributes found with net-based triads, cartels and terrorist entities. The characteristics of all three generations of gangs are summarized in Table 2.

The three generations of gangs can be described as follows:

Turf: First Generation Gangs are traditional street gangs with a turf orientation. Operating at the lower end of extreme societal violence, they have loose leadership and focus their attention on turf protection and gang loyalty within their immediate environs (often a few blocks or a neighborhood). When they engage in criminal enterprise, it is largely opportunistic and local in scope. These turf gangs are limited in political scope and sophistication.

Market: Second Generation Gangs are engaged in business. They are entrepreneurial and drug-centered. They protect their markets and use violence to control their competition. They have a broader, market-focused, sometimes overtly political agenda and operate in a broader spatial or geographic area. Their operations sometimes involve multi-state and even international areas. Their tendency for centralized leadership and sophisticated operations for market protection places them in the center of the range of politicization, internationalization and sophistication.

Mercenary/Political: Third Generation Gangs have evolved political aims. They operate—or seek to operate—at the global end of the spectrum, using their sophistication to garner power, aid financial acquisition and engage in mercenary-type activities. To date, most third generation (3 GEN) gangs have been primarily mercenary in orientation; yet, in some cases they have sought to further their own political and social objectives.

A more detailed discussion of these three generations follows.

First Generation Gangs
Traditional street gangs are almost exclusively turf-oriented. They operate at the lower threshold of extreme societal violence, possess loose leadership and concentrate their attention on turf protection and gang loyalty within their immediate environs (often a few blocks, a cell-block, or a neighborhood). When they engage in criminal activity, it is largely opportunistic and individual in scope. Turf gangs are limited in political scope, and are unsophisticated in tactics, means, and outlook. When they engage in rivalry with competing gangs, it is localized.

Despite their limited spatial influence, these gangs due to their informal network-like attributes can be viewed as proto-netwarriors. Local criminal organizations can evolve into armed bands of non- state soldiers should they gain in sophistication within failed communities with disintegrating social structure. While most gangs will stay firmly in the first generation, a few (e.g., some 'Crip' and 'Blood' sets and some Hispanic gangs) span both the first and second (nascent organized crime groups with a drug focus).

Second Generation Gangs

Second generation gangs are essentially criminal businesses. They are entrepreneurial in outlook and generally drug-centered. They use violence to protect their markets and limit or control their competition. They seek a broader, market-focused, occasionally overt political agenda and often operate in a broader spatial or geographic area. Their operations sometimes involve multi-state, cross-border, or international reach. They tend to embrace centralized leadership and conduct sophisticated operations for market protection. As such, they occupy the center of the range of politicization, internationalization and sophistication. Second generation gangs sometimes use violence as political interference to incapacitate enforcement efforts by police and security organs. Generally, this instrumental violence occurs in failed states, but clearly occurs when gangs dominate community life within 'failed communities.' Further evolution of these gangs is a danger when they link with and provide services to transnational criminal organizations or collaborate within narcotics trafficking and distribution networks and other criminal ventures. Because of their attributes, second generation gangs can be considered emerging netwarriors.

Third Generation Gangs

The overwhelming majority of street or prison gangs remain firmly in the first or second generations; however, a small number in the United States, Canada, Central and South America, as well as South Africa have acquired third generation characteristics. Third generation gangs have evolved political aims, operate or seek to operate at the global end of the spectrum, and employ their sophistication to acquire power, money, and engage in mercenary or political activities. To date, these gangs have been primarily mercenary in orientation; yet, in some cases they seek political and social objectives. Examples of third generation gangs can be seen in Chicago, San Diego, Los Angeles, Brazil, South Africa, and throughout Central America.

These gangs have evolved from turf-based entities, to drug-oriented enterprises operating in up to 35 states, to complex organizations controlling entire housing projects, schools and blocks, that conduct overt political activity while actively seeking to infiltrate and co-opt local police and contract security forces. These activities demonstrate the often-subtle interaction of gangs and politics. This shift from simple market protection to power acquisition is characteristic of third generation activity.

Internationalization is the final indicator of gang evolution. Gangs in Los Angeles and San Diego have been notable in this regard, with Los Angeles gangs having outposts in Tijuana, Mexico, Nicaragua, El Salvador, and Belize, and San Diego gangs linking with Baja cartels. The mercenary foray of San Diego's 'Calle Treinta' ('30th St.'/'Logan Heights') gang into the binational orbit of the Arellano-Felix (Tijuana) cartel is notable for assassinations, drive-by shootings and other enforcement slayings. Because of their attributes, third generation gangs can be considered netwarriors. Networked organizational forms are a key factor contributing to the rise of non-state or criminal soldiers.[13]

Impact of Transnational 'Third Generation' Gangs (Maras)

Like their more sophisticated cartel counterparts, third generation gangs challenge state institutions in several ways. Naval Postgraduate School analyst Bruneau, paraphrased below, describes five (multi) national security threats or challenges associated with transnational maras:[14]

- They *strain government capacity* by overwhelming police and legal systems through sheer audacity, violence, and numbers.
- They *challenge the legitimacy of the state*, particularly in regions where the culture of democracy is challenged by corruption and reinforced by the inability of political systems to function well enough to provide public goods and services.
- They *act as surrogate or alternate governments*. For example in some regions (i.e., El Salvador and Guatemala) the "governments have all but given up in some areas of the

capitals, and the maras extract taxes on individuals and businesses."

- They *dominate the informal economic sector*, establishing small busi-nesses and using violence and coercion to unfairly compete with legitimate businesses while avoiding taxes and co-opting government regulators.
- They *infiltrate police and non-governmental organizations* to further their goals and in doing so demonstrate latent political aims.

These factors can be seen graphically in the battle for control of the drug trade in Mexico.

The Plazas of Conflict

Mexico's drug wars are fertile ground for seeking an understanding of criminal insurgency. Mexico and the cross-border region that embraces the frontier between Mexico and the United States are embroiled in a series of interlocking criminal insurgencies.[20] These criminal insurgencies result from the battles for dominance of the 'plazas' or corridors for the lucrative transshipment of drugs into the United States. The cartels battle among themselves, the police and the military, enlisting the support of a variety of local and transnational gangs and criminal enterprises. Corrupt officials fuel the violence, communities are disrupted by constant onslaught of violence, and alternative social structures emerge. Prison gangs—like *Eme*, the Mexican Mafia—also play pivotal roles in the allocation of force and influence. Coping with these threats requires new operational and intelligence approaches.

Red teaming is one tool for understanding these "geosocial" dynamics. Looking at the influences, market imperatives, and factors that drive cartel and gang evolution, as well as the quest for dominance in the *plazas* helps place the violence encountered in criminal insurgency in context. In this analytical endeavor, red teaming is more than the tactical red cell penetration of vulnerable nodes. It is an adaptive exploration of the criminal enterprises and their interactions within the social and market dynamics of the plazas. This can be described as *analytical red teaming*.

Analytical red teaming looks at the network attributes of gangs and cartels in order to determine indicators for future activity. Which gangs or cartels are emerging in a particular area, what factors will extend their reach? Where are their new markets, what is the interaction between a specific gang or cartel? These intelligence questions can be explored through scenarios and analytical wargames. What factors are key market drivers? Where will new markets emerge? What counter-gang approaches will degrade criminal influences in failed communities? How can legitimate community political and social structures be marshaled to limit criminal reach and influence? By applying adaptive, analytical red teaming as an analytical tool, intelligence and law enforcement analysts can explore indicators of gang or cartel evolution, as well as potential courses of action to counter criminal insurgency.

Conclusion

Criminal organizations, particularly drug cartels and transnational gangs are becoming increasingly networked in terms of organization and influence. As these groups evolve, they challenge notions of the state and political organization. States are, at least in the current scheme of things, entities that possess a legitimate monopoly on the use of violence within a specified territory. Third phase cartel, criminal free state or criminal enclaves are factors that challenge that monopoly, much the same as warlords within failed states.

As previously discussed, the current situation in Mexico may shed light on these processes. Mexico is consumed by a set of inter-locking, networked criminal insurgencies. Daily violence, kidnappings, assassinations of police and government officials, beheadings and armed assaults are the result of violent combat between drug cartels, gangs, and the police. The cartels vying for domination of the lucrative drug trade are seeking both market dominance and freedom from government interference. Tijuana, Ciudad Juárez, and other border towns are racked with violence. Increased deployments of both police and military forces are stymied in the face of corrupt officials who chose to side with the cartels.

The drug mafias have abandoned subtle co-option of the government to embrace active violence to secure safe havens to ply their trade. This de facto 'criminal insurgency' threatens the stability of the Mexican state. Not satisfied with their feudal outposts in the Mexican interior and along the US-Mexico frontier, the cartels are also starting to migrate north to the United States and Canada and south throughout Central America, and even to the Southern Cone, setting up business in Argentina, and across the South Atlantic to Africa. Money fuels global expansion, and transnational organized crime has learned it can thrive in the face of governmental crisis.

The cartels are joined by a variety of gangs in the quest to dominate the global criminal opportunity space. Third generation gangs—that is, gangs like Mara Salvatrucha (MS-13) that have transcended operating on localized turf with a simple market focus to operate across borders and challenge political structures—are both partners and foot soldiers for the dominant cartels. Gangs and cartels seek profit and are not driven by ideology. But the ungoverned, lawless zones they leave in their wake provide fertile ground for extremists and terrorists to exploit.

Understanding and anticipating these threats is essential to maintaining social control, stability and effective governance. Criminal insurgency requires a new set of skills and organizational capabilities. Intelligence can help craft the understanding needed to build these. The cartel evolution and third generation gang models discussed her are useful analytical frameworks for developing this understanding.

On the operational side, full spectrum policing— that is community policing, investigations, high intensity policing (for gangs and organized crime), public order/riot control, counterterrorism, and counterinsurgency— must be developed and deployed. This will require versatile formed units like Israel's Joint Operations Forces (JOF). These are essentially stability police units (i.e., as gendarmerie/constabulary forces) such as an expeditionary police (EXPOL) or third force options.[21]

Finally, intelligence and operational art need to be closely integrated. A high degree of coordination and co-operation among government agencies and community groups at all levels of governance is needed.[22] This requires both police forces and intelligence services need to cooperate across borders[23] to gain understanding and achieve the 'co-production" of intelligence necessary to counter transnational criminal threats.[24]

Table 1. Phases of Cartel Evolution

1st Phase Cartel Aggressive Competitor	2nd Phase Cartel Subtle-Co-opter	3rd Phase Cartel Criminal State Successor
Medellín Model	Cali Model	Ciudad del Este/Netwarrior Model
Hierarchical Limited Transnational and Inter-enterprise Links Emerging Internetted Organization	Local (Domestic) Internetted Organization Emerging Transnational and Inter-enterprise Links	Global Internetted Organization Evolved Transnational and Inter-enterprise Links
Indiscriminate Violence	Symbolic Violence Corruption	Discriminate Violence Entrenched Corruption (Legitimized)
Criminal Use and Provision	Transitional (both criminal and mercenary) Use	Mercenary Use and Provision
Conventional Technology Use and Acquisition	Transitional Technology Use and Acquisition	Full Spectrum Technology Use, Acquisition and Targeting
Entrepreneurial Limited Economic Reach	Semi-Institutionalized Widening Economic Reach	Institutionalized Global Economic Reach
Small Scale Public Profiting	Regional Public Profiting	Mass Public Profiting
Limited "Product" Focus	Expanding "Product" Focus	Broad Range of Products/Activities
Criminal Entity Emerging Netwarrior	Transitional Entity Nascent Netwarrior	New Warmaking Entity Evolved Netwarrior

Source: Robert J. Bunker and John P. Sullivan, "Cartel Evolution: Potentials and Consequences," Transnational Organized Crime, Vol. 4, No. 2, Summer 1998.

Table 2. Characteristics of Street Gang Generations

limited	***Politicization***	*evolved*
local	***Internationalization***	*global*
1st Generation	2nd Generation	3rd Generation
turf gang	drug gang	mercenary gang
turf protection	market protection	power/financial acquisition
proto-netwarrior	emerging netwarrior	netwarrior
less sophisticated	***Sophisitication***	*more sophisticated*

Source: John P. Sullivan, "Third Generation Street Gangs: Turf, Cartels, and Net Warriors," Transnational Organized Crime, Vol. 3, No. 3, Autumn 1997.

CHAPTER 5

THIRD-GENERATION GANGS AND CRIMINAL INSURGENCY IN LATIN AMERICA

Hal Brands

Initially published July 4, 2009

IN MAY 2006, A previously obscure gang known as the First Capital Command (PCC) threw Sao Paulo into chaos. Over a period of five days, the PCC attacked hundreds of public buildings and private businesses, murdered policemen and civilians, and brought life in South America's largest city to a standstill. The scope of the violence clearly overwhelmed state and local authorities, and order was restored only after negotiations with the gang's leader, a man named Marcola. All told, the incident demonstrated that the PCC—rather than the government— effectively ruled large parts of Sao Paulo. As one Brazilian security official put it, "The sad reality is that the state is now the prisoner of the PCC."[1]

Roughly a year and a half earlier, another Latin American gang staged an even more shocking display of its power and ruthlessness. In December 2004, members of Mara Salvatrucha, or MS-13, stopped a bus in Chamalecon, Honduras, and proceeded to massacre 28 passengers. As Ana Arana relates, the killings were as notable for their apparent randomness as for their gruesomeness. "The slaughter had nothing to do with the identities of the people onboard; it was meant as a protest and a warning against the government's crackdown on gang activities in the country."[2]

Both the December 2004 incident in Honduras and the May 2006 attacks in Sao Paulo are part of a broader trend in Latin America: the rise of sophisticated, internationally-oriented, and extremely violent gangs. These "third-generation gangs," as they are often called, participate in the drug trade and myriad other illicit economies, and use violence and corruption to undermine the state. They increasingly straddle the line between crime and insurgency, and constitute a dire and growing threat to internal stability in the region. This phenomenon is most pronounced— and most remarked upon—in Central America, but it has spread well beyond the isthmus and now plagues countries from Mexico to Brazil.[3]

This essay offers an analytical framework for understanding third-generation gangs and the challenge they represent. It begins by examining the sources and characteristics of the gang problem in Latin America. It then considers the implications of gang activity for democratic government and internal stability in the region. It concludes with suggestions as to how the United States and its Latin American partners might go about addressing these threats.

Third-Generation Gangs and the Regional Context

Analysts generally divide gangs into three categories: first-generation, second-generation, and third-generation. First-generation gangs, which make up the largest of the three categories, are street gangs. They focus mainly on protecting their turf—normally no more than a few city blocks—from equally parochial rivals. Their criminal activities—assault, robbery, and petty extortion—are small-scale and opportunistic. First-generation gangs rarely have more than a few dozen members, and their organizational structures are horizontal rather than hierarchical. Second-generation gangs are larger and more complex (and thus less commonplace) than first-generation gangs. Frequently organized around illicit economies like drug trafficking, second-generation gangs operate across several cities or even internationally. They have links to transnational criminal organizations (TCOs) like drug cartels, and feature a more centralized leadership and a more hierarchical structure than first-generation gangs. Their violence is systematic and meant to protect or expand market share.

Third-generation gangs are sophisticated TCOs in their own right. They are complex, hierarchical organizations that operate according to a division of labor. While they participate in many of the same activities as first- and second-generation gangs, they operate on a grander scale. Third-generation gangs usually operate in more than one country, or at the very least have international alliances with other criminal groups. They control crucial nodes in a variety of illicit global networks: drug smuggling, arms dealing, money laundering, kidnapping, human trafficking, and others. Third-generation gangs are the rarest of the lot, occupying the highest part of a pyramidal gang hierarchy.

Most important, third-generation gangs stand astride the line separating crime and insurgency. These organizations go to such lengths to protect their highly lucrative economic activities that they end up undermining the authority and legitimacy of the state. They murder police officers, soldiers, and other authorities that try to interfere with their business; they infiltrate, corrupt, or otherwise weaken government institutions; they use intense, calculated violence to carve out geographic zones where they can dominate the population and operate completely free of state control. For the most part, third-generation gangs do this for profit rather than ideology,[4] but their actions are nonetheless deeply corrosive to state sovereignty, licit economic activity, and public security. In other words, while third-generation gangs often lack the explicit political agenda generally associated with insurgencies, their activities thus have many of the same political effects as an insurgency.[5]

Throughout the developing world, the post-Cold War era has seen a dramatic rise in both the prevalence and prominence of third-generation gangs. As Moisés Naím relates in his book, *Illicit*, criminal organizations have exploited some of the most important international trends of the past 20 years to achieve unprecedented wealth and influence. Economic and financial integration, innovations in communications technology, the rising number of weak and failed states, a thriving global arms trade, and the general erosion of national borders: These trends have created a "smuggler's nirvana," giving impetus to both massively profitable illicit commerce and the violence that inevitably attends it.[6]

Latin America has proven particularly vulnerable to this phenomenon. The region has porous borders, numerous illegal economic flows, and is awash with guns— all factors conducive to organized crime. Corruption is endemic and state institutions are weak, giving criminal organizations significant leeway to operate. Widespread poverty and social alienation ensure the gangs a steady supply of young recruits; densely packed urban slums give them near impenetrable havens in which to operate. Finally, in Central America especially, the deportation of tens of thousands of criminals from the United States over the past 15 years has effectively swamped law enforcement systems in countries like El Salvador and Guatemala.[7]

As a result, Latin America is now home to some of the world's most fearsome third-generation gangs. Central American *maras* such as MS-13 and M-18—rival gangs whose adherents are frequently marked by their elaborate tattoos—have tens of thousands of members spread across countries from El Salvador to Canada.[8] In Brazil, the PCC is one of several gangs that dominate the slums and prisons of the country's major cities. The PCC, which began as a prisoners' rights gang before diversifying its criminal portfolio, now has perhaps 100,000 members and maintains alliances with the Revolutionary Armed Forces of Colombia and mafia groups in Paraguay and Argentina.[9] In Mexico, the chaos surrounding the drug trade has given rise to groups like *Los Zetas*. Though the Zetas are a relatively small organization (they are estimated to have between 100-200 members, perhaps slightly more), they are now considered by U.S. officials to be "the most technologically advanced, sophisticated and violent" of the drug-related organizations active in Mexico.[10] The group has terrorized its opponents while carving out lucrative drug trafficking and distribution networks and cultivating relations with gangs in Central American and the United States. The list goes on; additional third-generation gangs can be found in countries throughout the region.

Characteristics and Methods

While third-generation gangs in Latin America vary dramatically in terms of size, history, and composition, all four of the groups discussed above—as well as a number of their counterparts— share several key characteristics. For one thing, their operations run the gamut of illegal activities. All of these groups derive significant income from drug trafficking and distribution, but they are also involved in a range of other enterprises—human smuggling, kidnapping, extortion, contract killings, arms dealing, and simple robbery. These various activities, in turn, require the gangs to dispose of vast sums of dirty cash, and they have therefore become key participants in the money laundering industry.

Latin American gangs can manage this broad portfolio because they are, in many cases, extremely well organized. These groups are no mere street gangs; they are complex organizations layered both vertically and horizontally. In MS-13, for instance, a top tier of transnational leaders provides direction to *clica* (local branch) bosses, who oversee several divisions responsible for enforcement, recruiting, propaganda, intelligence, finance, arms procurement, and other specific activities.[11] The Zetas operate according to a multi-tiered structure in which *La Dirección* (The Command) oversees the activities of relatively decentralized cells composed, variously, of teenage lookouts, intelligence-gathering prostitutes, former special-forces soldiers, and electronic surveillance specialists.[12] Brazilian gangs are just as complex; the PCC has a business and legal division in addition to cells tasked with performing many of the activities described above.[13]

As these descriptions indicate, most Latin American gangs boast a high degree of technological sophistication. The Zetas, for instance, employ computer experts to track the cell-phone signatures of their rivals and penetrate police and military communications channels. More generally, these groups use commercially available technology to coordinate strategy and operations. Central American *maras* have reportedly used satellite and cell phones to order assassinations, and Marcola, the leader of the PCC, directed the May 2006 attacks via cell phone despite being in solitary confinement in a maximum-security Brazilian prison. More audacious still, the PCC regularly holds conference calls that connect up to two-dozen leaders in various Brazilian prisons. Latin American gangs have also discovered the uses of the internet, employing web pages and chat rooms for recruiting and propaganda purposes.[14]

Above all, these gangs are extremely violent. In Mexico, Central America, and South America alike, third-generation gangs use a panoply of deadly weapons—heavy machine guns, rocket-propelled grenades, improvised explosive devices, sniper rifles, even crude armored vehicles— and strike with astounding brazenness and savagery. The Zetas and their Mexican competitors have assassinated hundreds of officials at all levels of government (including the chief of federal police) and frequently torture, behead, or immolate their victims. MS-13 and M-18 are just as vicious; they leave decapitated bodies in the streets and have in several cases massacred busloads of innocent travelers.[15]

This violence is sometimes described as senseless or random, but in fact it serves an essential political purpose. Waves of violence, whether directed at the authorities or at civilians, invariably come in response to government crackdowns on gang activity, and are coupled with warnings that future meddling will elicit even more violence. What the gangs are doing, in essence, is seeking to intimidate the state and the citizenry into submission and win a free hand in pursuing their lucrative business dealings.[16]

Across the region, gangs like the PCC, the *maras*, and the Zetas have taken this approach to the logical next step: using violence to carve out geographic areas where the government is essentially powerless to intervene. In cities in Mexico, Guatemala, El Salvador, and Brazil, gang violence has become so intense that the authorities have simply retreated from these areas, surrendering them to the gangs. The gangs then use these areas as free zones for drug trafficking, arms smuggling, and other illegal activities, and actually begin to exert their own perverse form of governance over the population. They collect "taxes" through extortion, and lay down a code of conduct for residents of the zone. Those who comply receive protection as well as limited social services like food, toys, and clothing; those who don't are entitled only to brutal punishment. Just as the Latin American insurgents of the 1970s and 1980s had their "liberated zones," the gangs now have their own domains where they—rather than the government—can dominate the population and impose a degree of "order."[17]

Violence is not the only method used to undermine state institutions; corruption also plays an integral role. Latin American criminals have long used the formula of *plata o plomo* (money or bullets) to corrupt government officials; third-generation gangs have become masters of this strategy. Confronted with the choice between an easy payout and a gruesome death, law enforcement personnel frequently opt for the former, and each week seemingly brings news of another gang-related corruption scandal. In Mexico, groups like the Zetas have bribed tens of thousands of officials, from beat cops to authorities at the highest levels of the attorney general's office, in return for information and protection. In Central America, numerous government ministries have fallen prey to corruption. The PCC actually prepares young recruits for civil service exams, funds political candidates, and thereby infiltrates its loyalists into strategic positions within government. The gangs are not just battering the state from without; they are also weakening it from within in.[18]

Implications for Internal Stability
and Democratic Governance

The effects of gang activity have been devastating for Latin America. Corruption is more pervasive than ever, and murder rates are alarmingly high. Drug and gang-related violence took nearly 6000 lives in Mexico in 2008, and Latin America has the highest murder rates in the world.[19] The region's youth murder rate—a key indicator of gang violence—was more than twice as high as that of any other region last year.[20] Swaths of territory in numerous countries have been rendered virtually lawless, public security has declined precipitously, and a pervasive sense of fear has spread among the population in parts of Mexico, El Salvador, Guatemala, Brazil, and other countries. "We are prisoners in our own homes," says one Mexican woman.[21]

Just as troubling, gang activity has driven down economic activity across the region. Intense internal violence scares off domestic and foreign investment, imposes high costs (such as paying protection money or hiring private security guards) on legitimate businesses, and forces governments to devote scarce resources to security rather than economic development or poverty alleviation. According to the Inter-American Development Bank, the economic costs of violence in Latin America may be as much as 14.2 percent of gross domestic product.[22]

The cumulative result of all this has been to create a serious legitimacy deficit for democratic governments in Latin America. The fact that many governments cannot protect their citizens, control large areas of their own territory, or maintain relatively trustworthy police and judicial institutions has led to intense popular disillusion in the region. Confidence in government and democracy is down region-wide, sparking well-grounded concerns that Latin America's young democracies are being hollowed out from within. "In many countries," reports the U.S. Agency for International Development (USAID), "high levels of crime provide the strongest justification in people's minds for a military coup."[23] Along these lines, El Salvador, Guatemala, and Brazil have all seen disaffected citizens and off-duty members of the security forces engage in vigilante violence against gang members in a manner reminiscent of the "death squads" of the Cold War. In other cases, residents of poor urban slums have simply thrown up their hands and welcomed the semblance of order that the gangs provide.[24] These trends simply reinforce the negative trends at work in Latin America, and hardly bode well for democratic stability in the region.

Policy Implications

There is no easy solution to the gang problem. Latin American gangs are often better armed than the police, and, due to past human rights violations, involving the military in domestic security matters raises a host of difficult political questions in many countries. Latin American authorities have also struggled with the fact that the transnational nature of gang activity means that no one country can grapple with this issue alone. At the structural level, moreover, the success of the gangs reflects a number of factors deeply embedded in regional politics and society. Endemic corruption and weak judicial institutions facilitate gang activities and vitiate the effectiveness of government crackdowns; rampant poverty and a lack of economic opportunity ensure a steady stream of recruits into the lower levels of these organizations.

These issues have so far frustrated many of the anti-gang initiatives deployed by Latin American governments. These initiatives—the counter-drug strikes launched by the Calderon government in Mexico, the *mano dura* (iron fist) programs in Central America, high-profile sweeps of gang-dominated slums in Brazil—have incarcerated tens of thousands of suspected gang members without providing any lasting solution to this challenge. In certain respects, *mano dura* programs are actually counterproductive, as locking up first-time offenders—the people who start at the lowest levels of these organizations but may eventually rise to the top—simply forces them to rely on their gang affiliations to survive in prison and thereby hardens gang loyalties.[25]

What is therefore necessary is a strategy that enhances internal security capabilities in Latin America while also addressing the underlying issues that fuel gang activity. On the former count, Latin American governments will need U.S. assistance in bolstering the forces of order. This means not simply upgrading the tactical capabilities of the police and other domestic security institutions. It also means helping Latin American countries develop intelligence sharing procedures and asset forfeiture laws, implement effective anti-gang legislation and asset forfeiture laws, and interdict cross-border drug and weapons flows. The United States and its Latin American partners have already put a number of programs in place to address these issues—interdiction programs in Central America, the Eastern Pacific, and the Caribbean, an international MS-13 task force, the Merida counter-drug initiative, and the Transnational Anti- Gang Unit, to name a few. Going forward, U.S. and Latin American officials must soberly evaluate the strengths and weaknesses of these programs so as to build upon successful initiatives and address potential shortfalls.[26]

On the latter count, Washington should assist in the formulation of initiatives meant to combat corruption, rehabilitate young gang members and first-time offenders, and ease the poverty and alienation that makes gang membership such an attractive option for young Latin Americans. Given the stubbornness of these problems, this often seems a Sisyphean task, but there are already a number of nascent programs that U.S. and Latin American officials can look to in this regard. In Mexico, the Calderon administration has had some success with creating small, specially vetted counter-drug units, and is pursuing a promising judicial reform. In Central America, the FBI and other agencies have begun to run personnel exchange programs meant to promote a culture of professionalism and respect for the rule of law. In El Salvador and Honduras, USAID has made some initial progress with programs that provide former gang members with micro-loans and vocational training. Finally, micro-lending and targeted social spending have helped reduce extreme poverty and increase school attendance in countries like Chile, Peru, Uruguay, and even Nicaragua. None of these programs are panaceas, but they do indicate ways that U.S. and Latin American officials might go about making sustainable progress in the fight against the gangs.[27]

Two decades after the end of the Cold War brought down the curtain on the brutal civil wars that roiled Latin America during the 1970s and 1980s, the region is once against beset by bloody internal upheaval. This time around, the culprits are sophisticated criminal gangs rather than Marxist guerrillas, but their rise threatens to be every bit as destructive as the insurgencies of an earlier era. Defeating third-generation gangs will require an integrated strategy that combines measures ranging from security assistance to social programs. Implementing such a strategy will be neither cheap nor easy, but the alternative—a lawless region where democratic governments cannot protect their citizens—would be many times worse.

CHAPTER 6

A VOLATILE BREW

Robert Killebrew
Initially published July 5, 2009

LAST JUNE A GROUP of men in police SWAT team uniforms stormed a building in Phoenix, Arizona, and killed a suspected drug dealer. But the gunmen wearing police uniforms and firing police weapons weren't cops— they were members of a Mexican drug gang evening scores with a troublesome dealer in the United States. When the real police arrived, the gang dug in for a shootout. That's increasingly common south of the border, but fortunately it didn't end well for the criminals this time.

The Phoenix incident is just one symptom of the growing unrest across the United States' southern border, where the Mexican government is waging a deadly war against murderous drug cartels. Even further south, a volatile brew consisting of thousands of demobilized former soldiers and guerrillas, state-sponsored terrorists and criminalterrorist hybrids such as the Revolutionary Armed Forces of Columbia (FARC) and the Salvadoran MS-13 gang is threatening the rule of law in Latin America. More ominously, it's moving north. In fact, some of these thugs are already here.

What we're talking about isn't just Mafia-style internecine warfare, or your local neighborhood gang showing off their new 9mms on the corner. The wave of criminality coming our way is a deadly and disciplined mixture of drug-fueled violence and terrorism, and it could erupt in the United States into a 21st-century insurgency not unlike the war now under way in Mexico.

I'm not being alarmist. Our understanding of the international gang picture is shadowy and filled with uncertainties, but it's clear that four trends that have been building for decades are coming together to threaten the peace and security of the places where we live.

First is the enormous growth of every kind of illicit traffic— in drugs, weapons, cash and human beings, among others— that has created a global black economy touching virtually every town, city and country in the world. The collapse of the Soviet Union, in particular, released vast entrepreneurial energies and materials for the black-market world. Huge dumps of weapons of all types went up for grabs; borders became porous, particularly in Southern Europe and the Balkans. Impoverished men and women have become human cargo for the sweatshops and red-light districts of the developed world. Weak states have become illegal free-trade zones for moving arms, money and enslaved humans. And the European and North American trade in illegal drugs has generated enormous profits for those skilled and ruthless enough to seize the opportunities the black economy offers.

Second, state-sponsored terrorist groups, most notably Lebanon's Hezbollah, have spread beyond the Middle East and Africa into Latin America. Hezbollah has long had a presence in South America, dating back at least to 1994, when the group was implicated in the bombing of a Jewish center in Argentina that killed 85. The election of leftist Hugo Chavez in Venezuela, and his establishment of friendly ties with Iran, gave the movement a state sponsor that could midwife its spread elsewhere in the region with transportation, false identities and dodgy Venezuelan passports.[1] In 2002, the State Department reported active Hezbollah cells in Venezuela. Iran's national airline, IranAir, now offers a weekly direct flight between Tehran and Caracas. In addition, there have been numerous reports that Hezbollah and al-Quaeda have set up fundraising shops together in South America's tri-border area between Argentina, Brazil and Paraguay, centered on the Paraguayan town of Ciudad del Ester.[2]

The threat of state-sponsored terrorists to our south is magnified by the third trend— the growth of guerrilla groups turned drug traffickers, such as the FARC, and of transnational gangs like MS-13, the 18th Street gang and others, which threaten the rule of law in some parts of Central America and have also established themselves throughout the United States and Canada, from Oregon to Florida, and in cities ranging in size from Los Angeles and Washington, D.C., to Charlotte, North Carolina and scores of smaller urban areas. Closer to home, law enforcement authorities believe that the Washington, D.C. area and Northern Virginia has the second-largest concentration of MS-13 in the U.S., after Los Angeles.[3] The gang traffics in drugs, extortion, kidnapping, theft and anything else that appears profitable. Loosely controlled from El Salvador, it enforces ruthless discipline by beatings and, for serious offenses such as informing, murder, often after unspeakable tortures. In 2005, Northern Virginia gang members were convicted of stabbing to death a pregnant 17-year-old named Brenda Paz after learning she was a federal informant.

Finally, the Mexican drug cartels, which sometimes employ MS-13 and other gangs as muscle, are in a class by themselves. A 2008 report by the Congressional Research Service estimates their criminal earnings to be between $8 billion to nearly $25 billion annually, and they are so powerful that they threaten the state's authority to govern.[4] In 2006, President Felipe Calderon initiated a campaign against them that has led to vicious reprisals. Thousands of Mexican law enforcement officials and civilians have been killed, with more than 5,700 deaths in 2008 alone. Outgunned Mexican authorities face vicious attacks from paramilitary gangs armed with the latest weaponry, much of it imported from the United States. Government officials have been assassinated in their offices, cars and homes; last May, gunmen shot and killed Edgar Millan Gomez, the acting head of Mexico's federal police, as he walked into his apartment. Torture and beheadings of police officers— taking a page from Al Queda in Iraq's reign or terror— are almost daily fare.

The U.S. response to all this at the national level has thus far been limited and grudging, consisting of the $1.6 billion multiyear Merida Initiative security agreement, negotiated between Calderon and President George W. Bush in 2007. Congress approved it last June, but only after attaching strings that the Mexican government found deeply insulting. Calderon's decision to take on the cartels was an act of great political and personal courage. Should he lose heart or be assassinated himself, we may wind up with a lawless nacre-state on our southern border.

Taken together, these four trends add up to what a military strategist would call an "indirect" assault against the United States. The opposition in this case isn't a foreign army or even insurgents on the Iraqi or Taliban model. Instead, these are brutal criminal terrorist hybrid networks out for profit, with no regard for national boundaries or governments. Through corruption and fear, they create "ungoverned spaces" where the rule of law is weak or nonexistent; they open the door for anarchy and murder and strike directly at the foundations of civil order, an environment in which terrorism thrives. The cruelest twist is that we are largely arming and funding them ourselves through the North American drug trade, which sends billions of dollars and arms south of the border each year.[5]

Developing an effective national response to this complex, and growing, threat will have to involve all government agencies, not just those normally associated with "traditional" security policy; fortunately, our ongoing experiences in Iraq and Afghanistan have taught us the necessity for a "whole of government" approach.[6] An integrated U.S. strategy could fall generally along these lines:

Because their security is tied so directly to ours, we should assist our southern neighbors, particularly Mexico, in developing or strengthening the institutions they need to protect their own sovereignty and enforce their laws. Congress should provide necessary funding, and rewrite Vietnam-era legislation that still restricts U.S. ambassadors and U.S. regional military commanders from assisting host countries to train and equip police and paramilitary forces.

The illegal movement of criminal gang members into the United States touches on U.S. border security and immigration policy. We should continue with enhancements already launched to safeguard our borders and provide funding to assist Mexican border police and the border police of other countries, as secure borders are in everybody's best interests. And we should proceed with comprehensive immigration reform, which the growth of transnational criminal gangs has made a national security issue. The large illegal Latino population in the United States often provides unwilling cover for criminal gangs because people are afraid to go to the police; fear of deportation makes also them easy prey for blackmail, extortion and violence by the same gangs.

Local police forces are the frontlines against MS-13 and other gangs, but they're frequently underfunded, too thin on the ground and often have difficulty coordinating quickly with other jurisdictions. What we need today is a sequel to the Clinton Administration's Community Policing Act of 1993, which put 100,000 new officers on the streets— many of whom were later let go when federal funding stopped. More police, better training and increased federal help for national data-sharing systems are important priorities.

Finally, this "war" against enemies in our midst should include social policies aimed at reducing drug use, treating those already hooked and reforming a system that warehouses small-time offenders with hardened criminals, virtually guaranteeing that they become thugs themselves. Here, and throughout the Americas, prisons have become "crime universities," and it must be stopped. A national drug treatment program— last seen in the Nixon Administration— is an urgent need.

Criminal gangs and terrorists are becoming inextricably linked in the shadowy world of international crime, and it is coming closer to your neighborhood. Given the precedence of the Phoenix incident, and others, Mexican cartels may soon begin assassination attempts against U.S. officials inside the U.S.[7] We've never seen a challenge quite like this, one that combines overseas threats with enemies in our own neighborhoods. It's past time for forceful, coordinated action at all levels of government to insure the safety of our own citizens and the survival of our friends.

CHAPTER 7

CARTEL V. CARTEL: MEXICO'S CRIMINAL INSURGENCY

John P. Sullivan and Adam Elkus
Initially published February 1, 2010

As THE DECADE ENDS, Mexico's criminal insurgency continues. Yet the narco-war in 2010 is not identical to the violence that began three years ago. Mexico's criminal insurgency at the beginning of 2010 is distinguished by three main trends: continuing (though increasingly diffused) violence against the state, increasing militarization of the Mexican state's response, and a growing feeling of defeat among some within Mexican policy circles. Additionally, the conflict has assumed broader transnational dimensions.

On the surface, the conflict has entered into a period of seeming stasis. But it is a bloody stalemate—and the war promises to continue simmering well into this year and beyond. According to the Mexican press, 2009 may have been the bloodiest year of the war, with 7,600 Mexicans perishing in the drug war.[1] Whatever the nature of the conflict, the danger still remains to American interests. As we have noted before, loose talk of a Mexican "failed state" obscures the real problem of a subtler breakdown of government authority and bolstering of the parallel authorities that cartels have already created.

All Against All

The government's strategy, essentially a 'war of attrition' is failing. The result of heavy-handed military action is the increasing 'fractilization' of the conflict, higher levels of violence, and increasing discontent by the general public and elites. Though the war has largely vanished from the mainstream American press after last summer's panic over the prospect of Mexico as a 'failed state,' the violence continues and risks of cross-border spillover remain. From the beginning, the criminal insurgency was never a unified project.[2] Cartels fought each other as well as the government for control of crucial drug smuggling routes, the plazas.[3] The fragmented and post-ideological quality of the struggle often confused American commentators used to the idea of a unified and ideological Maoist-type insurgency as the be-all and end-all of insurgency.[4] Yet the essential character of the insurgency is something that Clausewitz, were he around today and tuning into gangster-promoting *narcocorrido* music pumping out of Tijuana radios, could definitely understand.[5]

The Mexican government under President Felipe Calderón had elected to use force to crush the parallel states built up by cartels. The cartels decided to use force to accomplish the policy of thwarting the Mexican response. Adding to the violence was the internal competition between the cartels themselves for valuable drug-smuggling real estate, aided in part by corrupted sectors of the government that captured by the cartels.[6] This is the basic genesis of the conflict, although the political and economic issues that contribute to and sustain it go back much further.[7]

Yet as the level of violence increased, the conflict has grown progressively less coherent. Where attacks once mainly focused on the state and other drug smuggling competitors, more and more attacks seem directed at civilian populations and more local in scope and origin. In part, some of this violence is the result of leadership vacuums, local turf wars, and the difficulty of controlling violent and reckless junior henchmen. However, it also seems the inevitable result of the escalation of the conflict, which has ripple effects on lower-order crime and violence. Slums have become war zones, with drug gangs recruiting discontented and impoverished youth to become foot soldiers over turf in such slums as Ciudad Juárez's Barrio Azul.[8]

As the war shifts local and regional power dynamics among cartels, power struggles expand and up-and-comers struggle with established criminal powers. Sadly typical of the low-level violence that increasingly characterizes the conflict was the apparently random death of an El Monte, California educator at the hands of unknown gunmen in the small town of Gomez Palacio.[9] Longtime Latin America watcher Samuel Logan, for example, notes that even *Los Zetas*, the former military unit turned cartel enforcer group, has become larger and less professional.[10]

Competition between groups can also be expressed through government action, as cartels have captured lower-level military and law enforcement arms. Journalist Philip Caputo argues provocatively that the Mexican drug war is a civil war between cartels and their government clients rather than the government and the cartels.[11] In a way, this is the inevitable result of the government's heavy crackdown, as it throws military and police elements and their families into direct temptation and coercion by cartels. In this manner, the conflict has become even more diffused and dangerous for the average Mexican.

As we emphasize the diffuse character of Mexican violence, we should not overemphasize its random nature. Even as the violence grows progressively more random, the central target for many groups remains the government. The government's goal is to destroy the cartels as political entities within Mexico and to expand state power to the parallel zones of sovereignty dominated by cartels. This is the reason why cartels fight as hard as they do, because they are fighting for their basic livelihood and existence against both the government and their competitors at the same time. They cannot back down.

Counter-Cartel Surges

The main vehicle for government control is the use of federal police and increasingly the military. The thinking of the government is essentially tactical, consisting of "surges" of troops to stabilize or 'pacify' violent areas. Ciudad Juárez, for example, is essentially an occupied city with a garrison of 7,000 soldiers and 2,000 federal police. As a *Wall Street Journal* report details, however, the killings continue unabated. By some estimates, Juárez's 165 deaths per 100,000 residents make it the murder capital of the world. Soldiers patrol but do not stay for long outside of their bases, for fear that extended contact with locals will induce desertions or defections to the higher-paying cartel organizations.[12] Mexican military tactics consist almost exclusively of raiding, hoping to win a war of attrition with the cartels.

Problems that face Mexican military units engaged in drug action are very similar to those encountered in modern counterinsurgencies such as Iraq and Afghanistan: a population too cowed by the enemy to cooperate, enemies hiding among the populace, and hit and run attacks by squad-sized enemy units. Intelligence issues also are a perennial problem. The trend of cartel soldiers engaging in pitched battles with weapons ranging from bazookas to anti-aircraft guns has been a constant of the conflict, Juan David Leal notes in an article for *El Diario*. Cartels also routinely attack prisons to liberate arrested prisoners.[13] They routinely launch grenade attacks on police garrisons and army bases, and aggressively attack patrols with the tenacity of guerrillas.[14]

The state of the drug war in Ciudad Juárez is emblematic of the dilemma facing the Mexican state. Consider the impact of the military and the corresponding impact of the conflict on the military. According to the aforementioned *Wall Street Journal* feature:

> The chaos in Ciudad Juárez has snared Mexico's army, the country's most respected institution, in what may be a no-win situation. Even as the violence rises, so do allegations of human rights abuses by the army. The failure to pacify Ciudad Juárez has put Mr. Calderón's antidrug strategy—based largely on using the military to retake control of the country from drug cartels that have corrupted local police and politicians—on embarrassing public display.[15]

Counterinsurgency (COIN) approaches are an attractive option for the Mexican state. According to Cordoba and Millman:[16]

> Some experts say the Mexican army needs to adopt the style of the counter-insurgency tactics used by the U.S. military in the Iraq war. That strategy got American soldiers out of large bases and forced them to interact with the population and get intelligence. 'They have to co-mingle with the locals and find out who's who in the zoo. Find out where the bad guys are, and preempt them,' says a former U.S. military officer with knowledge of the Mexican army. But, the official says, the Mexican army, which is made up of conscripts, isn't trained on how to interact with the community. The result: a lot of patrolling that's good for show but bad for results.

Certainly, COIN has applicability since the Mexican drug war is part 'criminal insurgency' part 'high intensity crime.' However, more is needed. Integrated police, military, and intelligence operations are required, but community policing and conventional crime suppression must be emphasized over military approaches. This is also true in mainstream COIN, but even more critical in counter-drug, counter-gang, and criminal insurgencies.

The complexities of utilizing the military to restore domestic social control require additional research and examination. In Mexico, the reliance on military forces to curb the cartels and their extreme violence has led to accusations of human rights abuses. For example, Amnesty International, citing cases of alleged slayings by the military in the drug war, criticized civilian officials, saying they fail to properly investigate or prosecute crimes by the army. The Mexican army, deployed across Mexico as part of the government's campaign against drug cartels, has been accused of killing prisoners, torturing civilians and capturing suspects illegally.

In its report, *Mexico: Human Rights Violations By The Military*, Amnesty International (AI) accuses the authorities of failing to fully probe allegations of abuses committed by the military, including enforced disappearances, extrajudicial and unlawful killings, torture, ill treatment and arbitrary detentions. The AI report says the number of human rights abuse claims in Mexico has more than tripled from the beginning of 2008 through June of this year compared to the previous two years.[17]

Human rights are not the only concern. Communities besieged by narco-cartels often are also under siege from street gangs and more mundane criminals. State emphasis on cartel activity that ignores community policing has negative impacts on social stability. The resulting absence of security helps strengthen the hand of the cartels and erode the legitimacy of the state. Mexican authorities are currently recognizing this dilemma; for example, KPBS reports:

"Tijuana Mayor Jorge Ramos has given his police chief a new assignment this year: to focus on common crime. According to Ramos, common criminal activity in Tijuana has increased recently, 'Since we're fighting drug lords in the city. But our main responsibility is to fight the robberies and that kind of crime in the city, so that's going to be our main object this year.' The report notes that '[s]ome crime watchers and people in Tijuana's business sector have complained that Tijuana's police force has left large swaths of the city unprotected while police battle organized crime.'"[18]

The situation in Tijuana highlights the importance of sustaining security and countering crime in conflict zones. After a sweeping review of the military's two-year occupation of Ciudad Juárez, officials concluded that the deployment of thousands of soldiers against drug traffickers has failed to control the violence and crime. As a result, police (albeit trained in urban combat) will soon replace the army as the primary security force. According to Reuters, the Mexican army, "facing accusations of rights abuses, will give federal police control of security in [Ciudad Juárez] the country's most violent drug war city even as cartel killings escalate."[19]

The dynamics of *intraconflict* policing demand more than COIN. Full-spectrum policing which uses some COIN approaches, integrates community policing, intelligence-led policing/intelligence preparation for operations to allow complex investigations. Together with corruption control, these form the foundation for the capacity to contain high-intensity violence and managing criminal insurgency. The key is developing an appropriate police capacity that can leverage the military for support rather than relying on the military as the core security force.

Unfortunately, Mexico's police do not have the skills. Police reform must be accelerated or the military will increasingly lose their effectiveness.[20]

Since both existing police and regular military forces are severely challenged and at risk of being co-opted by the cartel gangsters, regular forces are increasingly augmented by specialized units drawn from the Navy. The employment of elite naval forces offers the advantages of higher levels of training, and quicker reaction times. In addition, the Navy is perceived as being more loyal than the increasingly cartel-penetrated Army and police forces. They are being utilized to essentially carry out decapitation raids against high-level cartel figures. This is another element of the attrition strategy.[21] By targeting high-level figures, the Mexican government seeks to fatally weaken the cartels. Leadership targeting can be part of a counter-cartel strategy, as Colombia in the

1990s demonstrates. But it is not sufficient as the main effort of a counter-cartel strategy.

This has been demonstrated by the effect of the killing of Arturo Beltrán Leyva, head of Beltrán Leyva Organization (BLO). Navy special forces killed the drug lord to great fanfare and press attention. The drug organization reacted swiftly with brutal reprisals, including the murder of a fallen Mexican Marine's family.[22] In this case, *La Jornada* reported:

> 'Criminal groups with their firepower and powers of corruption are waging a determined battle to subjugate the country' according to Mexican President Felipe Calderón. 'We will not step back from this fight' and there will be no truce and no quarter to the enemies of our country,' he said.[23]

Just hours after Calderón declared there would be "no quarter and no truce" in the war with criminal organizations, gunmen from a suspected BLO-Zetas commando team killed the mother and four relatives of a Navy Special Forces (Marine) sergeant who died in the raid in Cuernavaca that killed Arturo Beltrán Leyva. The BLO allied with the Zetas in 2008. Needless to say, another member of the BLO swiftly took Leyva's place.[24] The Leyva killing has also had effects on a long-running struggle between the Sinaloa Cartel, lead by Joaquín "El Chapo" Guzmán, and the Juárez Cartel and its leader, Vicente Carrillo Fuentes. Both are struggling for control over the lucrative Juárez *plaza*.[25]

The Rise of Mega Cartels?

Megacarteles? The shifting alliances of Mexican drug cartels in face of their war with each other and the state appears to have the potential of resulting in two competing alliances or 'megacartels.' According to *Excélsior*, SEDENA (the Mexican intelligence agency) considers this prospect in a report "S1P1."[26] The assessment states that eight drug trafficking organizations in Mexico have united to form two solo groups in order to gain control of drug trafficking and its associated routes in the country. The breakdowns of these alliances were reported as follows: 1) The Sinaloa Cartel headed by Joaquín Guzmán Loera, "El Chapo," has aligned with La Familia Michoacana, the remnants of the Milenio/Valencia Cartel, and with a faction of the Tijuana Cartel. 2) The second block consists of the Beltran Leyva organization, the Juárez Cartel, Los Zetas, and the Tijuana Cartel.

The first alliance has been reportedly forged by Sinaloa Cartel leaders Ignacio Coronel Villarreal *aka* Nacho Coronel who reputedly brought La Familia Michoacana and Los Valencia onboard, and Ismael Zambada García *aka* "El Mayo." Zambada was responsible for negotiations with Teodoro García Simental, "El Teo" (before his arrest).[27] The second alliance was reputedly the result of efforts by Arturo and Hector Beltrán Leyva who met with Miguel Trevino Morales to form an alliance with the Gulf Cartel/Los Zetas. This was then approved by Heriberto Lazcano Lazcano aka "El Lazca." The Beltrán Leyva brothers also are alleged to have established the alliance with Vicente Carrillo Fuentes *aka* "El Viceroy."

In addition to the potential two dimension alliances, the SEDENA report also speculates that the Gulf Cartel and Los Zetas are in the process of splitting. According to the report, Los Zetas have become an independent faction of the Gulf Cartel, so much so that among themselves, they no longer identify each other with the letter "Z," but rather, with the letter "L."

The potential result of this new alliance formation is accelerated battle between the two megacartels as each of the new groups seeks to decimate the other and take over their respective trafficking routes, plazas, and territories. Higher levels of executions, extreme violence, and terror are likely. The states of Sinaloa, Coahuila, Chihuahua, Nuevo León and Tamaulipas are now under the control/influence of the Juarez Cartel, the Beltrán Leyva Organization (BLO), and the Gulf Cartel/Los Zetas. An all out war against the Sinaloa Cartel and their armed group, La Gente Nueva may be germinating.

Add to this the prospect that a US national, "El Tigrillo" a South Texan may be in line to become the next BLO drug king. Edgar Valdez Villarreal, "a 36-year-old U.S. citizen born in South Texas, has gone from high school jock to potential Mexican drug cartel boss— perhaps the only U.S. citizen to do so," according to the *San Antonio Express-News*. Valdez, known as "El Tigrillo" and "La Barbie," was a close confidant of Beltrán Leyva Organization (BLO) cartel boss Arturo Beltrán Leyva, who was killed in December. While it's still unclear who will succeed Beltrán Leyva, Houston DEA officials speculate that if Valdez Villarreal takes the reins of BLO it's likely he will renew the feud with Gulf Cartel bosses on the Texas-Mexico border.

The prospects of this protean dynamic—the interaction of violent competition, fragmentation, morphing, and amalgamation—are likely to involve continued extreme violence and barbarization. The cartels and their enforcer gangs will continue to adapt and shift organizational form in an effort to gain and maintain control. This will result in continued attacks against the police and military, each other, and from time-to-time, journalists, judicial officials, politicians, and the public at large.

These conditions, unless countered, will exacerbate the existing "hollowing" of state capacity and fuel the growth of "parallel polities." Criminal enclaves will dominate some segments of Mexican states. These will likely be slums (*barrios* and *colonias*) and loosely patrolled border zones. Security sector reform, along with strengthening of the police and democratic institutions within Mexico's states is essential to counter the cartels and the potential human rights abuses that occur when combating them without a complete array of appropriate governmental capabilities.

Some policy elites are wearying of President Calderón's escalation of the drug war. Former officials from the Vicente Fox administration Ruben Aguilar and Jorge Castañeda have written a book titled *El Narco: La Guerra Falida* (Narco: The Failed War) that harshly attacks the drug war and instead emphasizes a focus on reducing violence overall.[29] The publication of the book is significant, and shows the growing controversy surrounding the drug war.

Lastly, the international context of the conflict cannot be ignored. Drug- trafficking in Mexico has repercussions in Central America, the overland route for supply since the interdiction of the Caribbean route. Violence in nations such as Guatemala has sadly become endemic, as drug smuggling issues mesh with local political and social ills. Mexican cartels have expanded their reach throughout Central America, across the Atlantic into West Africa, and as far south as the Southern Cone. They are also present in the US—and not just in border cities. While their criminal reach is broad, the bulk of their warfighting is currently occurring in Mexico. It must be contained there. Although the cartel war is *mainly* a US-Mexico problem, it is not exclusive to either nation; it is a regional security issue.

Conclusion

Future potentials for the conflict are difficult to extrapolate, given the impact of Mexican domestic politics on the conflict. However, if support continues to hold for Calderon's policy, the conflict is likely to continue for the next year on its present course. Law enforcement will continue to be phased out and military approaches, including special forces high-value targeting, will continue to become the main effort of Mexican counter-drug policy. In turn, the competition over cartel real estate will become more hectic and the cartel war will continue to fractalize.

The consequences for US border communities if such a state of affairs continues are a worsening of local crime as cartel violence and competition spirals out of control. Moreover, as we have previously argued, the stability and security of our southern neighbor is a basic national interest.

The current US policy investment in the war is the Merida Initiative. As Hal Brands notes, the military aspects of the Merida Initiative are positive—better equipment, ISR (intelligence, surveillance, and reconnaissance) abilities, and intelligence sharing will improve the operational proficiency of Mexican striking forces.[30] Yet interdiction, arrests, and other tactical issues are not the whole of the problem. Brands also observes that money for anti-corruption initiatives, judicial reform, human rights training for law enforcement, and other societal issues is decidedly absent from the Merida Initiative.[31] Nor is there anything aimed at poverty alleviation that could stem cartel recruitment. Demand-side reduction in the United States is also absent.[32]

United States policy must embrace a different approach. This should include a strategic review of both US counter-narcotics policy and the threat of transnational organized crime. This review must be comprehensive and consider a range of options. This cannot be a unilateral effort; rather, it should be carried out in consultation with the entire US interagency community (military, diplomatic, development, economic, law enforcement, and intelligence), and include state and local officials in both US and Mexican border states. It must also emphasize consultation with regional partners and non-governmental organizations. The second step is to choose a manageable goal.

Finally, police and 'rule of law' reform are key elements in developing a stable, secure society and countering the insidious impact of organized crime, gangs, 'criminal insurgencies,' and corruption. Mexico must continue its efforts to reform its police and justice system, ensuring transparency and effective enforcement that sustains state legitimacy and the security necessary for healthy communities free of crime and violence.

The United States cannot change Mexico overnight, nor would Mexicans allow us to do so if we could. At the same time, Mexico clearly cannot deal with the problem on its own, so some level of assistance is warranted. But it is possible for the US and Mexico in collaboration to cut the cartels down to a size that does not threaten government power. Such a goal could be accomplished through a combination of 'soft' measures such as judicial reform, government institutional development, law enforcement and military capacity building, and emphasis on human rights instruction with, 'hard' measures such as the Mexican Marine direct action missions that Mexico is already embracing.[33]

CHAPTER 8

CRIMINAL INSURGENCIES IN THE AMERICAS

John P. Sullivan

Initially published February 13, 2010

Transnational criminal organizations and gangs are threatening state institutions throughout the Americas. In extreme circumstances, cartels, gangs or maras, drug trafficking organizations, and their paramilitary enforcers are waging *de facto* criminal insurgencies to free themselves from the influence of the state.

A wide variety of criminal gangs are waging war amongst themselves and against the state. Rampant criminal violence enabled by corruption and weak state institutions has allowed some criminal enterprises to develop virtual or parallel states. These contested or "temporary autonomous" zones create what theorist John Robb calls "hollow states" with areas where the legitimacy of the state is severely challenged. These fragile, sometimes lawless zones (or criminal enclaves) cover territory ranging from individual neighborhoods, *favelas* or *colonias* to entire cities—such as Ciudad Juaréz—to large segments of exurban terrain in Guatemala's Petén province, and sparsely policed areas on the Atlantic Coast of Nicaragua.

As a consequence, the Americas are increasingly besieged by the violence and corrupting influences of criminal actors exploiting stateless territories (criminal enclaves and mafia-dominated municipalities) linked to the global criminal economy to build economic muscle and, potentially, political might.

Criminal Insurgencies

Criminal insurgency is different from classic terrorism and insurgency because the criminal insurgents' overarching political motive is to gain autonomous economic control over territory. As Professor Steven Metz noted in his monograph *Rethinking Insurgency*, not all insurgencies conform to the classic Leninist or Maoist models. Not all insurgents seek to take over the government or have an ideological foundation. Some seek a free-range to develop parallel structures for profit and power. Nevertheless, they have a political dimension, using political maneuvering and instrumental violence to accomplish their economic goals. As such they are insurgents—albeit of a criminal variety.

Mexico is a case in point. Imploding in a series of interlocking 'criminal insurgencies' culminating in a virtual civil war, kidnappings, assassinations, beheadings, and shoot-outs are commonplace. Since 2006 over 16,000 murders have been attributed to the drug war. Chihuahua, Sinaloa, Guerrero, Baja California, Michoacan, Sonora, Durango, Nueva Leon, and Tamaulipas are the states hardest hit. In Chihuahua, the violence continues to surge despite the presence of 7,500 military and 1,000 federal police. In some cases, the cartel gangs, like La Familia Michoacana, are embracing a social and political agenda to further their reach.

La Familia is engaged in combat with the Gulf cartel, Los Zetas, the police, and the Mexican state itself. In coordinated attacks against police conducted from 11 to 15 July 2009 La Familia demonstrated its resolve. La Familia dramatically emerged on the public scene in September 2006 when 20 masked gangsters stormed the Sol y Sombra nightclub in Uruapan, firing shots into the air and tossing 6 bloody and severed heads onto the dance floor. The intruders then left a cardboard placard or *narcomanta* elaborating their ethos, "The family doesn't kill for money. It doesn't kill for women. It doesn't kill innocent people, only those who deserve to die. Know that this is divine justice."

Combining religious fervor, propaganda and the mantle of "social bandit," La Familia has capitalized on both reputation and myth to secure power and reach. It is a regional polydrug/poly-crime organization with its fingers in methamphet-amine, marijuana, and cocaine trafficking, kidnapping for ransom, and pirated CDs and DVDs—not to mention co-opting politicians and nurturing political control and influence. Their banditry and violence are tools for inspiring support and sympathy from a community that feels abandoned and powerless.

One of their rivals, Los Zetas, is formed from a core of former Mexican special forces soldiers. Initially aligned with the Gulf Cartel, they have morphed into a cartel in their own right. Los Zetas operate across Mexico's northern and southern frontiers, aligning themselves with various gangs and private armies. Similar to La Familia, they evoke religious, cult symbolism—in this case the cult of Santa Muerte—to forge social bonds and cohesion. Like La Familia, they also use extreme violence, beheadings and brutality to secure their reign. Other cartels including the powerful Sinaloa cartel, and the Beltran-Leyva organization complete the vicious circle, competing for control of Mexico's lucrative transshipment "plazas" and trafficking corridors.

Collectively, these cartels and their enforcer gangs—which amount to virtual private armies— threaten the stability of the state. A top-ranking Mexican intelligence official, CISEN director Guillero Valdes noted that criminal gangs pose a national security threat to the integrity of the state. Cartels have co-opted police, local mayors and politicians, and have even tried to take over or co-opt the Mexican Congress by funding political campaigns.

Cartels and Gangs in Central and South America

The impact of such high intensity violence becomes more than a localized criminal issue. Transnational gangs and crime have hemispheric and global potentials. Criminal insurgents are incubators of instability that leverage globalization. As a consequence transnational or global crime is changing the nature of war and politics throughout the Americas. Guatemala and Honduras, Panama and Costa Rica, indeed all Central America, are currently at risk of being caught in the "cross-fire" of the region's drug wars. The cartels are joined by a variety of gangs in the quest to dominate this global criminal opportunity space. Third generation gangs—like Mara Salvatrucha (MS-13) and Brazil's urban drug gangs that have transcended operating on localized turf with a simple market focus to challenge political structures—are both partners and foot soldiers for the dominant cartels. In addition, traditional insurgents like the Revolutionary Armed Forces of Colombia (FARC) engage in criminal enterprise to fuel their activities and make alliances of convenience with other gangsters.

Some states like Costa Rica, Panama, and Nicaragua are not only shifting from drug transit to processing territories, they are becoming drug-consuming nations themselves. Drug gangs are a consequence, in turn stimulating a rise in crime and violence. In Guatemala, Mexican drug gangs are exploiting proximity, weak law enforcement and deep-rooted corruption to expand their reach. For example, the Zetas have carved a bloody trail across Guatemala's northern and eastern provinces over the past year and a half.

Guatemala under the Gun

More than 6,000 people were slain in Guatemala in 2008. Police say most of the killings were linked to the drug trade. An analysis from the North American Congress on Latin America assesses the military threat to Guatemala from Los Zetas. According to the report, "vast parts of the country are under Zeta control." Carlos Menocal, a top security adviser to President Colom, believes that the Zeta bases discovered in Guatemala were created not just to aid in smuggling, but to be used to defend their territories militarily. These Zeta bases are believed to use Kaibiles to train a range of gangsters including *mareros* from MS-13. The *Latin American Herald Tribune* reports that Guatemala has suffered 2,953 murders during the first nine months of 2009. An additional 1,179 people were injured in violent incidents during the same period.

Brazil's Feudal Favelas

Over 5,000 people were murdered in Rio de Janeiro last year, in a battle between rival drugs gangs and militias. Rio's parallel gang state co-exists with the legitimate government. For example the Terceiro Comando Puro (Pure Third Command) essentially governs the *favela* of Parque Royal, deploying its own cadre of community organizers to mediate conflicts and dole out favor. Alfredo Sirkis, a prominent Rio politician, noted in a recent media interview that "Rio is one of the very few cities in the world where you have whole areas controlled by armed forces that are not of the state." In Rio's *favelas*, the state is almost completely absent. The drug gangs impose their own systems of justice, law and order, and taxation enforced through force of arms. Military-issue machine guns and anti-aircraft weapons, semi-automatic assault rifles and hand grenades are increasingly commonplace. According to Sirkus, "It [is] like a Middle Ages phenomenon, feudalism and warlordism without any purpose other than living day to day...It's a low-intensity, non-ideological insurgency."

Conclusion: Impact and Response

The globalization of economic processes has empowered a new class of "global criminals" including criminal insurgents. These "criminal netwarriors" are a serious impediment to democratic governance and a free market economy. Efforts to control the scope and reach of high intensity criminal violence and "criminal insurgency" are necessary to sustain stable communities and democracy. State security forces, primarily the police supported by the military and intelligence services, must work together to contain the violence while empowering legitimate political processes. This coordination and interoperation must cross borders and leverage regional security cooperation and reform throughout the Americas.

CHAPTER 9

THE SPIRITUAL SIGNIFICANCE OF ¿PLATA O PLOMO?

Pamela L. Bunker and Robert J. Bunker
Initially published May 27, 2010

CONVENTIONAL WISDOM HOLDS THAT narco gang and drug cartel violence in Mexico is primarily secular in nature. This viewpoint has been recently challenged by the activities of the La Familia cartel and some Los Zetas, Gulfo, and other cartel adherents of the cult of Santa Muerte (Saint Death) by means of religious tenets of 'divine justice' and instances of tortured victims and ritual human sacrifice offered up to a dark deity, respectively. Severed heads thrown onto a disco floor in Michoacan in 2006[a] and burnt skull imprints in a clearing in a ranch in the Yucatán Peninsula in 2008 only serve to highlight the number of such incidents which have now taken place. Whereas the infamous 'black cauldron' incident in Matamoros in 1989, where American college student Mark Kilroy's brain was found in a ritual nganga belonging to a local narco gang, was the rare exception, such spiritual-like activities have now become far more frequent.

These activities only serve to further elaborate concerns amongst scholars, including Sullivan, Elkus, Brands, Manwaring, and the authors, over societal warfare breaking out across the Americas.[1] This warfare— manifesting itself in 'criminal insurgencies' derived from groups of gang, cartel, and mercenary networks— promotes new forms of state organization drawn from criminally based social and political norms and behaviors. These include a value system derived from illicit narcotics use, killing for sport and pleasure, human trafficking and slavery, dysfunctional perspectives on women and family life, and a habitual orientation to violence and total disregard for modern civil society and democratic freedoms. This harkens back to Peter's thoughts concerning the emergence of a 'new warrior class' and, before that, van Creveld's 'nontrinitarian warfare' projections.[2]

A recent insight, gained by the authors after the conclusion of a major research project on Mexican drug groups,[3] is that this insurgency has at its basis a spiritual, if not religious, component that threatens the underlying foundations of our modern Western value system. This component is derived from the well known cartel technique of offering an individual *¿Plata O Plomo?*—take our silver or we will fill you with our lead. As a tactic taken by groups with a theological bent, such as La Familia, this offer becomes Faustian, join us and in the process give up your soul or die, a choice historically associated with incidents of religious conversion at the tip of a sword. That technique is typically carried out by young religions, such as militant Christianity and Islam, during their expansionistic phases. These post-battlefield mass conversions are considered by the victors as actually saving the souls of those joining the righteous ranks of God's chosen. A side benefit of such practices is of course to replenish the ranks of the fallen and to vastly increase the size of a religious movement via an ever-expanding holy war. Compare the size and power of Islam in the 7th century to that of the religion a couple of centuries later and the historical benefits of this process become readily apparent. Even Christianity, with Emperor Constatine's conversion prior to the Battle of the Milvian Bridge in the early 4th century, has benefited from a similar process with the subsequent mass religious conversion of the Roman state and its legions.

In the context of the Mexican cartels, and to a more limited extent the earlier Colombian ones, what we are now witnessing is a process in which criminal conversion by the bullet is taking place. This is an allied concept to that discussed by Manwaring with regard to the 'Sullivan-Bunker Cocktail' that targets state sovereignty by eating away at institutions of a state.[4] Individuals targeted by the *¿Plata O Plomo?* Cartel technique can either choose to embrace criminality by taking the bribe offered or be killed. While individuals are allowed 'free will' and can choose death with a clear conscious over that of embracing criminality, Hobbes typically has a clear advantage over Rosseau when the final decision is made. Thus, in accepting the bribe, such individuals, while they preserve their own skins, readily compromise their values and join what is becoming a growing criminal insurgency in the Americas against the modern Westphalian state system. No moral salvation exists for those who cross the line and accept the silver of the narcos. Corruption taints the soul and we are increasingly finding ourselves besieged by growing ranks of such lost souls with their Cuerno de Chivo (Goat's Horn— AK-47 assault rifle) talisman in hand.

Yet, what is still missing in this conversion equation is a strong and overarching religious archetype or movement that helps to more fully unite those embracing the criminality espoused by the narco gangs, cartels, and their mercenary foot soldiers. La Familia adherents, while dramatically increasing, now only number less than ten thousand while the far more numerous cult of Santa Muerte, now ranging in number somewhere between one and five million, has more of its followers thought to still subscribe to the older and more benign forms of that religious practice. This suggests that we are nowhere near a tipping point where criminal conversion also corresponds to some sort of threatening or dark form of narco related religious conversion. What it does suggest, though, is as the *¿Plata O Plomo?* conversion technique continues to be refined and increasingly spreads in Mexico, Central America, regions of South America, and penetrates over the United States border with Mexico, it prepares the ground and creates fertile conditions for such narco spiritual potentials.

An example of this concern is that of a Los Zetas assassination cell composed of US teens working in Laredo, Texas in the 2005-2006. One of its members, hitman Gabriel Cardona, sported a large Santa Muerte tattoo on the back and open eye tattoos on his eyelids that have helped to elevate him to a 'narco mark of the beast' archetype. Religious shrines and altars, which include the burning of black candles and a few instances of blood sacrifices, have now also been tied to more extreme narco religious followers.

Honest men are increasingly accepting bribes and embracing criminality over certain death, in some instances, along with the threat of the infliction of torture. Such is the reality of day-to-day life in many of the sovereign free and cartel controlled zones that now exist in Mexico and Central America. Who can say if those who are willing to compromise their values—and in a sense have already darkened their souls—are not willing to complete the transformational process taking place and accept criminally derived forms of spirituality and religion into their hearts? In the war over social and political organization now raging in the Americas, we must expect and prepare for these and other such contingencies.

CHAPTER 10

EXPLOSIVE ESCALATION? REFLECTIONS ON THE CAR BOMBING IN CIUDAD JUAREZ

John P. Sullivan

Initially published July 21, 2010

IN AN APPARENTLY SIGNIFICANT acceleration of tactics, techniques and procedures (TTP), Mexican cartel violence embraced the car bomb in an attack on Federal police in embattled Ciudad Juárez last Thursday, 15 July 2010. Not only did the attack employ a car bomb (apparently a primitive improvised explosive secreted inside a car not the fully-integrated variant found in Iraq, and the AfPak theatres known as a VBIED), but it also was an ambush that directly targeted police. This TTP is a classic insurgent attack method that promises to be part of Mexico's future engagements in its on-going criminal insurgencies.[1]

The Car Bomb in Ciudad Juárez

News reports claim that four persons were killed in what is described as a well-planned, "bait and wait" trap near a Federal police facility. This attack is the first documented use of a car bomb by drug traffickers or their affiliated gangs since the start of Mexico's counter-cartel offensive. Clearly the use of bombs (ranging from simple IEDs— improvised explosive devices—to the more complex large vehicle bomb— LVB—

erstwhile known as a VBIED— vehicle-borne explosive device) portends to dramatically alter the nature of Mexico's drug wars. Until this assault, cartels and their paramilitary gangsters have relied on small arms (including assault weapons such as AK-47 variants known as the *'Cuernos de chiva'* or goat's horn after their magazine), limited use of grenades, and symbolic beheadings to neutralize competing gangster and government security forces.

While barbaric beheadings, bold small arms attacks (active shootings), and the occasional grenade or combined small arms-grenade attack are a challenge to police, the potential specter of urban car bombings — with their attendant casualty generating capacity — poses a threat similar to the darkest days of narco-violence in Colombia or the insurgencies in Iraq and Afghanistan. A *'narcomensaje'* or message left at the scene claimed the Juarez Cartel was responsible for the blast, and it threatened further attacks. "We still have car bombs," said the alleged warning.

According to the Associated Press, the *'La Linea* drug gang — the same group blamed for the March killing of a U.S. consulate employee and her husband — lured federal officers and paramedics to the site of a car bomb by dressing a bound, wounded man in a police uniform and calling in a false report of an officer shot.... The gang then exploded a car holding as much as 22 pounds (10 kilograms) of explosives, killing the decoy, a rescue worker and a federal officer. A regional military commander said a cell phone might have been used to detonate the bomb." More recent reports suggest the device employed Tovex, an industrial explosive.[2] Now, it appears this was a simple car bomb, yet not a fully-evolved VBIED. That said, VBIED is an extremely jargon-laden term. The sophistication or operational effectiveness of the device is only one element of the attack and shouldn't be over conflated with the TTP or delivery platform. Recall, "Buda's Wagon" (the first modern "car" bomb)[3] wasn't sophisticated in terms of what we see in Iraq, AfPak theaters either, but was still a car bomb. This device appears to be a transitional weapon, where cartel bomb makers are experimenting and importing TTP from other conflicts to exploit on their own battleground. We can be thankful this device was primitive, but should expect them to remedy their short fallings as the conflict evolves.

In the same report, Cd. Juárez Mayor Jose Reyes Ferriz said authorities "will have to change the way we operate. We've started changing all our protocols, to include bomb situations." A Mexican Brigadier (BG) Eduardo Zarate, the commander of the regional military zone, said as much as 22 pounds (10 kilograms) of explosives might have been used in the attack, adding that burned batteries connecting to a mobile phone were found at the scene. Clearly that challenges police responders.

In the words of Ferriz, "The threat was directed at the police departments, so it is not a threat against the population...But we have to be very careful with our police departments, their actions and how we protect them, and of course, how we protect the population from the fallout."[4] As a recent AP report noted: "While Mexican federal police have training in post-blast investigations, no security force in the country has experience with patrolling cities that could be mined with car bombs or roadside explosives."[5] The same is true of police here in the US and worldwide.

Grenades and car bombs escalate Mexico's strife

Mexico's criminal insurgencies appear to be escalating with not only the use of car bombs as well as hand grenades apparently stolen from military arsenals. Clearly, grenades are not new in the Mexican narco-war. Remember Morelia, 15 September 2008 when Suspected members of Los Zetas drug gang tossed grenades into a crowd celebrating Mexico's independence, killing eight people and wounding more than 100.[6] It was the conflicts first and only (thus far) attack on a mass gathering of civilians.

Nevertheless, according to the *Washington Post*, there have been more than 72 grenade attacks in Mexico in the last year, including spectacular assaults on police convoys and public officials. In addition, Mexican forces have seized more than 5,800 live grenades since 2007. This is reportedly a small fraction of a vast armory maintained by the drug cartels. The Prosecutor General of the Republic (PGR), Mexico's attorney general's office, claims that there have been 101 grenade attacks against government buildings in the past 3 1/2 years. Reports claim that the majority of grenades have been traced back to El Salvador, Guatemala, Honduras and Nicaragua, according to investigations by agents at the U.S. Bureau of Alcohol, Tobacco, Firearms and Explosives and their Mexican counterparts. In addition, grenades of Asian or Soviet and Eastern European origin are in play.[7]

'Narcopinta' warns of future car bombs

A GRAFFITI MESSAGE (*"NARCOMENSAJE"* or *"narcopinta"*) on a Cd. Juárez wall warns of a car bombing if US authorities do not look into alleged ties between Mexican federal police and drug traffickers. According to a Mexican official "Yes, another 'narcopinta' was spray-painted on a primary school wall Sunday night," Jacinto Seguro, a spokesman for the Juarez Municipal Police said. "It threatens another car bombing in 15 days if the DEA and FBI don't investigate the federal police ties to El Chapo [Guzman of the Sinaloa Cartel]."[8] While we can't over estimate the value of this threat, it is worth taking heed. The conflict will continue, and it is escalating. The use of information operations and threats is part of the operational environment, but not all propaganda is deception. It is likely the cartels and their gang affiliates will continue to target police, and perhaps civilians, as they seek to eradicate their rivals and secure free space to operate with impunity. Rather than discount this threat, we need to develop intelligence to accurately gauge evolving capabilities and intentions.[9]

Dissecting the Potentials

The Cd. Juárez car bombing attack occurred about 1930 hours near the intersection of Bolivia and 16 de Septiembre streets in Juárez's downtown district. First, what appeared to be a municipal police officer was shot and killed, and when Federal police and EMS responders arrived to the scene there was an explosion. An ambush employing deception (or surprise) was unleashed on patrol personnel. Here we see the need to emphasize IED awareness and force protection. Police responders frequently respond well to familiar threats—that is ballistic and human threats. They respond according to their experience and training. Grenade and IED (roadside and vehicle bombs) are largely outside their experience (in the US, Mexico, and in reality most of the world). Metropolitan police in the US are rapidly integrating active shooter training into their skill set. This training should (and does) include awareness of explosive threats (grenades, IEDs, and military munitions). With repeated exposure and practice, police can integrate a three-dimensional approach to situational awareness and threat response.[10] All too frequently, responders fix on the immediately apparent threat, engage gun fire, and in the natural "tunnel vision" that results under combat stress, miss non-ballistic threats and threats from other vantage points. This facet of close quarters battle can be corrected in tactical training and drills. Such efforts are essential. These include active shooter and IED awareness drills, drill on rescuing downed officers, and integration of force protection for emergency medical and fire service responders. In addition, this requires training and recognition of command post and crime scene defense capabilities.

Responding to infantry-like battles in rural areas is increasingly common in the Mexican drug war; translating that experience into urban criminal combat operations adds several magnitudes of complexity. In the urban operational space, not only do you face a determined adversary, but urban terrain in complex, three-dimensional settings (with subways stations and high rises, not to mention densely concentrated non-combatants and operational challenges). Beyond these tactical dimensions is the need for operational coordination and synchronization. Addressing multiple, simultaneous combined arms assaults (i.e., small arms and bombs) requires a degree of sophistication that challenges police worldwide.

Conclusion

These potential high intensity/criminal insurgency attacks demand real-time intelligence support, and superb tactical and operational command, control, and communications, all of which require new doctrine, training, and equipment. Essentially, we are seeing the need for "intra-conflict" policing employing "full-spectrum policing" where police can quickly shift from individual community policing duties into a formed unit (contact or fire teams and squads for close quarters battle) for tactical engagements against an armed, and organized opposing force.[11] These capabilities are needed in Mexico, throughout Latin America and here in the US (as well as in Europe, Australia and other nations where the police will undoubtedly face insurgents or terrorists of many stripes).

Such 'hybrid' skills would benefit from enhanced law enforcement-military interaction for assessing emerging conflict, developing tactical and operational doctrine, and cross training. It is not simply a matter of bringing counterinsurgency (COIN) skills to the police service, but rather a reciprocal exchange of knowledge and experience to address 'inter-conflict policing' where community policing and COIN converge to address the intersection of crime and war. At the strategic level, there is a need to define the role of police-military interaction for convergent threats such as transnational organized crime, criminal insurgency, and crime in conflict zones. This may require new force structures (such as expeditionary police), as well as integrating existing capacities (such as formulating the traditional DIME—Diplomatic, Intelligence, Military, and Economic—as DIME-P, adding the police service).[12]

Building an adaptive response capacity to address urban terrorist tactics employed in high intensity crime, criminal insurgencies whether they occur in Mexico, Latin America,[13] or further abroad in the Afghanistan, Pakistan or the Iraqi theatres is essential. This requires more than EOD or bomb squad responses, explosives awareness must be integrated into all police and emergency (fire/EMS) response at the general service (patrol, first response) levels here and in the nations currently challenged by conflict. The lessons learned in countering IEDs in Iraq and Afghanistan,[14] and now Mexico, must be shared and integrated into evolving public safety doctrine and emerging police operational art.

CHAPTER 11

THE US STRATEGIC IMPERATIVE MUST SHIFT FROM IRAQ/AFGHANISTAN TO MEXICO/THE AMERICAS AND THE STABILIZATION OF EUROPE

Robert J. Bunker

Initially published October 6, 2010

A Plea to the Barack Obama Administration and Both Houses of Congress.

THE UNITED STATES CURRENTLY faces two strategic level non-state (network) threats—but only one of them is openly recognized. Al Qaeda, and other elements of radical Islam, have been recognized as the #1 threat since the 11 September 2001 attacks which killed nearly 3,000 Americans and caused well over 100 billion dollars in infrastructure damage, emergency response, and economic disruption. This threat which garners ongoing media attention, however, on many fronts pales in comparison to that represented by the drug cartels and narco-gangs which for decades now have been evolving, mutating, and growing in capabilities and power in the Americas. While presently viewed as a 'crime and law enforcement issue', as Al Qaeda was pre 9-11, this more subtle and encompassing strategic threat has resulted in the deaths of well over 100,000 citizens of the Americas (roughly 30,000 in Mexico alone in the last 4 years) and has caused the destabilization of a number of nations including Mexico, Guatemala, and Honduras, and witnessed the rise of heightened narco influence within regions of the US homeland along its Southern Border. Economically, the sustained damage and disruption caused by drug cartel and narco-gang activities to private individuals, local economies, and governmental bodies is well past the trillion dollar mark and rising. Both of these non-state (network) threats challenge the institutions of the many nations affected, the loyalty of the indigenous populations to the state itself, and are indicative of the 'war over social and political organization' now being waged in various regions of the globe.

The 9-11 attacks resulted in the invasion of Afghanistan and Iraq by US and coalition forces. In hindsight, it can be agreed that the invasion of Afghanistan was a strategic necessity while the invasion of Iraq had nothing to do with the 9-11 attacks and can be chalked up to the foreign policy failings of a prior administration. What can also not be disputed is that the intent of these operations has politically shifted over time into the abyss of nation- and democracy-building exercises supported by mercenary forces and marred by domestic tribal power politics and the rampant corruption of autocratic rulers. The imposition of 'democracy by the sword' on tribal cultures and attempts at wholesale societal-engineering is imprudent even in best case scenarios. The cold reality that we face in these conflicts is that the US is hemorrhaging money, wearing out its forces, and enriching the pockets of corrupt tribal leaders and mercenary corporations. We, as a nation, cannot sustain these campaigns without wrecking ourselves as a great power in the process. The revenues simply do not exist, our national debt and the interest servicing it is mounting, and the opportunity costs of ignoring the Americas and our European allies are too high. It is time to accept that our best course of action is to simply render Afghanistan (along with Western Pakistan) and Iraq safe enough so as not to threaten the American and European homelands, accepting that this may result in competing tribal zones of interest in the former. Following this guideline, the US should phase withdraw its resources, both economic and military, from Afghanistan and Iraq at the earliest opportunities as it refocuses its strategic attentions.

The drug cartels and narco-gangs of the Americas, with those in Mexico of highest priority, must now be elevated to the #1 strategic threat to the United States. While the threat posed by Al Qaeda, and radical Islam is still significant, it must be downgraded presently to that of secondary strategic importance. Europe, due to the threat derived from changing demographics, larger numbers of citizens radicalized, and proximity to Islamic states, many of which contain Islamist insurgent forces, will continue to identify the threat of radical Islam as their #1 strategic imperative and should be allowed to take the opportunity to share, if not take the strategic lead, in this important area of concern. The recently heightened tensions in Europe with the threat of Mumbai style attacks directed at a number of its capital cities are indicative of the mandate which should now be provided to allied states such as Great Britain, France, and Germany and that of the more encompassing European Union. The US must help defend the line in Europe against terrorist attack, the imposition of Sharia law, and other threats to the social organization of our allies such as the disenfranchisement of women, while acknowledging for the immediate future, we have ignored for too long a new type of threat which has arisen far closer to home.

The US has unknowingly found itself in a multi-front war with two strategic level non-traditional threats that are not states. While Islamic prison radicalization is taking place domestically, some African American gang members have joined the Jihadist cause, numerous Al Qaeda affinity active shooter incidents have taken place, and Somali immigrants recruited in the US and operating back in their own nation as suicide bombers have been evident, the levels of radicalization and the recruitment pool potentials vis-à-vis those in Europe are presently still quite low. On the other hand, shifting demographics inside the United States, via both legal and illegal immigration from Mexico, has resulted in a relatively youthful Mexican-American (citizen) and illegal Mexican (non-citizen) population now in the 25-30 million range and rising. Virtually all the border zones of California, Arizona, New Mexico and Texas, including the major cities within them, have majority populations of Mexican ancestry. As these demographics increase within American society, and projections suggest they will, the fates of Mexico and the US become increasingly intertwined. While terrorism and violence is always of concern, including that utilized by Al Qaeda and affiliates in attacks against the West, a far more dangerous issue is that of threats to US institutional stability. It must be recognized that at present the dominant threat to the US homeland is the potential for corruption of its institutions by the Mexican cartels and narco gangs followed, in tandem, by cross-border violence spillover. The use of the *¿Plato O Plomo?* (Silver or Lead) insurgency technique of creating shadow cartel operating structures that hollow out local governmental authority within a region has proven exceptionally effective in many states of Mexico— including a focus on the plazas along the US border. While the US is well prepared to stand up to acts of violence directed against it, the utilization of Mexican cartel 'violence-corruption' techniques brings in a new element that makes it a larger and presently more insidious threat than that posed by Al Qaeda and its radical Islamic associates.

To date, the levels of corruption of US public agents appear not to have significantly increased and although the active investigation of corruption is increasing so too are the number of US Customs and Border Protection (CBP) and US Immigration and Customs Enforcement (ICE) officers now deployed. Regions of Arizona and Texas have armed cartel operatives positioned throughout the countryside with local police chiefs recently publicly stating that violence has officially crossed into the United States. Further violence and corruption potentials must be considered in the context of Mexican drug cartel and narco gang penetration into the US. As early as 2008, over 195 US cities had Mexican narco gang distribution and enforcement units situated within them. This is in addition to the expanses of marijuana fields controlled and defended by the cartels in Western US states and the domestic Mexican street and prison gang drug contractor network which numbers somewhere between 50,000 and 100,000 Sureños (Sur13), Tango Blast, Azteca, and related gang members.

In addition to threats to the American homeland, the domestic security posture and vitality of the Mexican state, and those of other Latin American nations also affected by narco corruption and violence, is of increasing concern. Parts of Mexico have been lost and may or may not now be regained. The same can be said for regions in Central America as well as for Colombia, whose decades long wars with insurgents, cartels, and gangs is still far from over. Ultimately, the United States must create an 'organizing hemispheric strategy' to contain the drug cartel and narco-gang threat. This was one of the policy recommendations discussed in the *Narcos Over the Border* (Routledge) manuscript finished in 2009 and echoed in the recently released *Crime Wars: Gangs, Cartels, and U.S. National Security* (Center for a New American Security). Such a comprehensive Hemisphere Defense Plan for the Americas would take into consideration the new forms of war and conflict now taking place in the early 21st century. In one sense, it would represent an update and modification of the early 19th century Monroe Doctrine and extend its prerogative to encompass non-state, network, and indigenous threats to the Americas. The United States of America must take the lead, focus necessary national elements of power, and help to coordinate the activities of allied American states to contain and combat what are basically 'new war-making entities' evolving in the New World. Such a strategy must also include community building at home and the provision of the necessary economic resources to create sustainable and accountable gang programs—something the city of Los Angeles and many other major urban zones in the US have failed to do time and again with ultimately haphazard and politicized initiatives.

Time is of the essence in this matter. No defining 9/11 incident is expected to take place in the near term concerning the drug cartel and narco-gang threat to the Americas which would galvanize the American public and its government. In fact, we can expect further Al Qaeda and affinity terrorist attacks to take place in Europe and the United States that will grab media headlines and further obscure, downgrade, and relegate the far greater cartel and gang threat to the media shadows. In retrospect, Mexico would have had a far better chance against the cartel and gang threat if it had acted years prior to going on the offensive in 2006 —though it still vehemently denies the truth and is unable to publicly state, because of national pride and hubris, that it is facing criminal insurgencies within its borders.[1] To call what is taking place in Mexico the actions of organized crime is delusional and as relevant to contemporary thinking as viewing the present-day world through the prism of the Cold War. The Mexican government made a strategic mistake and is paying for it on a daily basis with a domestic war that is far from over. The intensity of the conflict is increasingly more difficult to gauge with the ability to engage in free speech (reporting) across much of Mexico now disappearing, given the ongoing suppression and cooption of its news media. If the US government significantly delays in doing the right thing and does not shift its strategic imperative to addressing the rampant problems of Mexico and the Americas, including in the border regions of our own homeland and in enclaves within our major metropolitan zones, along with ongoing stabilization of Europe against the radical Islamic threat, we too as a nation will pay for it dearly in the years to come.

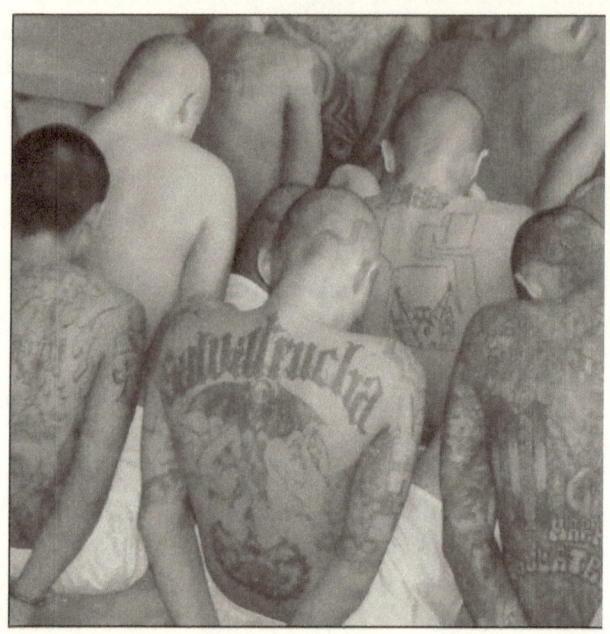

Figure 1: Incarcerated MS 13 Gang Members Source: 2011 National Gang Threat Assessment (NGTA) (For Public Distribution)

**Figure 2: Los Zetas Commando Medallion
Source: ATF (For Public Distribution)**

Figure 3: Weapons recovered from Barrio Azteca Members in Ciudad Juarez, Mexico Source: ATF (For Public Distribution)

CHAPTER 12

CRIMINAL INSURGENCIES IN MEXICO: WEB AND SOCIAL MEDIA RESOURCES

Robert J. Bunker and John P. Sullivan
Initially published January 12, 2011

THE AUTHORS OF THIS piece, individually, collectively, and in cooperation with other scholars and analysts, have written about the criminal insurgencies in Mexico and various themes related to them in *Small Wars Journal* and in many other publications for some years now. The *Small Wars* publications alone include "State of Siege: Mexico's Criminal Insurgency," "Plazas for Profit: Mexico's Criminal Insurgency," "Cartel v. Cartel: Mexico's Criminal Insurgency," "The Spiritual Significance of ¿Plata O Plomo?," "Explosive Escalation?: Reflections on the Car Bombing in Ciudad Juarez," and "The U.S. Strategic Imperative Must Shift From Iraq/Afghanistan to Mexico/The Americas and the Stabilization of Europe." Certain truths have become evident from such writings and the raging conflicts that they describe and analyze.

First, the criminal insurgencies in Mexico have been increasing in intensity since the formal declaration of war—penned with the initial deployment of Army units into Michoacán and Ciudad Juárez against the insurgent gangs and cartels—by the Calderón administration in December 2006. Over 30,000 deaths in Mexico, just over ten-times the death toll from the 9-11 attacks, have now resulted from these conflicts with 2010 surpassing the earlier end of year tallies with almost 13,000 total killings.[1] While most of these deaths have been attributed to cartel on cartel violence, an increasing proportion of them include law enforcement officers (albeit many of them on cartel payroll), military and governmental personnel, journalists, and innocent civilians. While some successes have been made against the Mexican cartels, via the capture and targeted killings of some of the capos and ensuing organizational fragmentation, the conflicts between these criminal groups and the Mexican state, and even for neighboring countries such as Guatemala, is overall not currently going well for these besieged sovereign nations. Recent headlines like those stating "Mexico army no match for drug cartels"[2] and "Drug gang suspects threaten 'war' in Guatemala"[3] are becoming all too common. Further, it is currently estimated that in Mexico about 98% of all crimes are never solved—providing an air of impunity to cartel and gang hit men and foot soldiers, many of whom take great delight in engaging in the torture and beheading of their victims.[4]

Second, *Small Wars Journal* readers, especially those in the United States, need to appreciate the strategic significance of what is taking place in Mexico, Central America and in other Latin American countries, and increasingly over the border into the United States itself. War and insurgency in Iraq, Afghanistan, Western Pakistan, and in other distant OCONUS locales ultimately represent much lower stakes[5] than the high levels of strife, establishment of criminal enclaves and depopulated cartel security zones, and rise of narco-cities—such as Nuevo Laredo under the Cártel del Golfo (CDG)—now taking place on our Southern border and extending down through Central America. A chilling example of the criminal insurgencies being waged is the fate of the contested city of Ciudad Juárez—over 230,000 people have fled, primarily the business elite and skilled workers; 6,000 businesses have closed, and tens-of-thousands of homes now stand vacant or have been abandoned.[6] While Ciudad Juárez may represent an extreme form of urban implosion, this pattern is being repeated in numerous towns throughout Mexico with many such towns and small villages in Northern Mexico now partially or fully abandoned and, even in some instances, burned to the ground.[7] To add insult to injury, some of the cartel conflict now taking place in the urban plazas and rural transit routes is being described in an almost post-apocalyptic manner with make shift armored pickups and even a ten-wheeled armored dump truck able to carry ten enforcers and with the combatants engaging in firefights with high caliber and anti-tank weapons.[8] It must now be accepted that the cartels and gangs of Mexico, Central America, and increasingly South America have morphed from being solely narcotics based trafficking entities to being complex, diversified criminal organizations. These criminal enterprises are increasingly politicized and armed with military grade weaponry, backed up with the training and esprit de corps necessary for them to make war on sovereign states. This asymmetric war now being waged is derived from their unique and evolving criminal insurgency tenets using not only the bribe and the gun but also, information operations,[9] and increasingly, deviant forms of spirituality in order to further dark and morally bankrupt agendas.

Web and Social Media Resources

It is with these truths in mind that the need for informed insight for U.S. law enforcement, military, governmental, and policy makers concerning these criminal insurgencies, is the reason that this short piece has been written. It provides an overview of the more useful and informative web and social media resources, in both English and Spanish that exist concerning this homeland security and hemispheric threat to the United States, Mexico, and many other countries extending south into Latin America. Not only do these resources outline the contours of Mexico's criminal insurgencies and drug war, but they also illuminate the influence of the new communications space (horizontal communications) on the conflict environment. As Tracy Wilkinson reported in the *Los Angeles Times*, "journalists are under siege," causing reporters to "practice a profound form of self-censorship, or censorship imposed by the narcos."[10] As a result, many reports assert that social media, Twitter, YouTube, and blogs—such as *El Blog del Narco*—are taking the place of traditional media. Wilkinson notes, "Social media networks such as Twitter have taken the place of newspapers and radio reports, with everyone from security officials to regular people tweeting alerts about a gun battle here, a blockade there."[11] As a consequence of the battle to control information, journalists, the public, and the cartels themselves have embraced "new media" technologies (*i.e.*, social networking sites, Twitter, blogs, and other forms of horizontal mass self-communication). These resources are as follows: Text marked with * is directly quoted from web and social media sites for accuracy.

Blog Del Narco (http://www.blogdelnarco.com): This Spanish language blog has received notoriety for filling the gap caused by narco-censorship. It was established in March 2010 and reportedly receives close to four million hits per week. It includes current reports, YouTube videos, and a forum. It maintains a Facebook page and Twitter account (@Infonarco). Graphic photos and comprehensive, timely coverage make it not only an excellent reference site, but also an important source for indications and warning (I&W) for placing emerging threat streams into context. *Información acerca del narcotrafico* (Information about narcotrafficking). **En Español/Resource in Spanish.**

Borderland Beat (http://www.borderlandbeat.com/): This is a comprehensive site with good imagery and information and useful links. Earliest blog postings began in mid-2009. Seven contributors are listed for this site which also contains a Twitter feed (@Borderlandbeat) and Facebook social plugin. *This blog is a reflection of the issues affected by crime and drugs along the border between Mexico and the U.S. It gives a perspective of issues related to the complicated issues of both neighboring countries and how the activities from one side impact the other. It is important for both sides of the border to understand how mayhem and ruthless violence from organized crime touches the people on the borderland and the misery it brings to every day social conditions we sometimes call civilization. Consider this a huge source of information related to crime on the borderland. Knowledge is power. *Info provided: Most of the information and content is derived from open source media, unconfirmed individual sources, and personal viewpoint of the author. Most content is for information purposes only and is not from direct official sources and, in most cases, is not confirmed. Some content is graphic and discretion is advised. Anonymous contributions and donations solicited.

Border Reporter (http://borderreporter.com/19/): This site was established in December 2005 and is administered by an organized crime reporter focusing on the U.S.-Mexican border and the activities of the Sinaloa Federation. The site carries lead stories, limited photos and videos, hot documents, and recent news along with field productions, investigations, and resource links and archives. The site accepts donations and also contains a Twitter feed (@borderreporter), Facebook social plugin, and other media links. *BorderReporter.com, specializes in intelligence and analysis from the border, uncovering government malfeasance and feature stories from the region not covered by other media. As an expert on border issues, he [Marizco] won several regional and state awards for his work along the Arizona-Mexico border. Stories appearing on *The Border Report* are regularly cited by national news media, from *CNN* to the *Dallas Morning News*, *El Universal*, and *Proceso* magazine. Marizco is available for freelance assignments. He lives in Tucson, Arizona.

CASEDE (http://www.seguridadcondemocracia.org): The Mexican research site is maintained by the Colectivo de Análisis de la Seguridad con Democracia A. C in Mexico City. Essentially a think tank, the Collective's president Raúl Benítez Manaut is an eminent Mexican academic and long-time analyst of Mexico's narco-conflict. Other notable SMEs include Jorge Chabat and Luis Astorga. The site covers crime and public security in Mexico. In addition to access to recent reports and publications (books, monographs, working papers), it has archival reports and statistics on crime in Mexico and maintains research links to Mexican resources, and a virtual library with sections on drugs and narcotrafficking, organized crime, and the Mérida Initiative. *En Español/Resource in Spanish.*

Gabriel Regino (http://www.gabrielregion.com): The Spanish language site is maintained by a Mexican lawyer. It provides analysis and insight into public security and cartel activity in Mexico. It also maintains an extremely valuable Twitter feed (@gabrielregino). Coverage on Mexican crime and cartels is excellent! A good I&W resource. *Abogado, Académico y Twitero* (Lawyer, Academic and Twitterer). *En Español/Resource in Spanish.*

GroupIntel (http://www.groupintel.com/): This open source intelligence site seeks to serve as a catalyst for collaborative analysis and the "co-production of intelligence." It contains a public blog and a members' only collaborative space. The public blog contains several essays on the Mexican situation including "Frontlines of Criminal Insurgency: Understanding the Plazas" and "Santisma Muerte: A Troubling Trend in Radicalization." The members' only "GroupIntel Network"(http://network. groupintel. com) contains 150 discussion threads including: "Mexico's Criminal Insurgencies," Transnational Organized Crime and Gangs," "Guatemala Under the Gun," "Expanding Cartel Reach,"

"Energy Security and Resilience" (including discussion on PEMEX attacks and resource extraction), "Police Reform in Mexico and Latin America." In addition to the discussions, several specialty groups including "The Rise of the Vigilante," "Boyd, 4GW Theory, and Criminal Insurgency," and "Terrorism Early Warning" round out the site, which also includes individual member blogs and collaborative research tools.

InSight—Organized Crime in the Americas (http://www.insightcrime. org/): InSight Crime is a virtual think tank. Its website became active in December 2010. The organization was founded in April 2010, under the auspices of the Fundación Ideas para la Paz (FIP) in Bogotá, Colombia, and with funding from the Open Society Foundations. In August, American University's Center for Latin American and Latino Studies became a sponsor. InSight currently has offices at the FIP in Colombia and at American University in Washington DC. The site contains news, investigations, group profiles, and a crime map. It also maintains a Facebook page and a Twitter feed (@InSightCrime). *InSight's objective is to increase the level of research, analysis and investigation on organized crime in Latin America and the Caribbean. To this end, InSight has created this website where it connects the pieces, the players and organizations and gives a cohesive look of the region's criminal enterprises and the effectiveness of the initiatives designed to stop them. InSight's staff also writes analysis and does field investigations, providing the type of on-the-ground research absent in other monitoring services.

Internet Resources for Latin America (http://lib.nmsu.edu/subject/bord/ laguia/): Provided by New Mexico State University and Molly Molloy, who tracks the Ciudad Juarez narco killings, this is an invaluable research site. The links on this site include selected current events contained in English and Spanish publications including *Frontera Norte Sur* and *Reforma*; Latin American web directories; subscription and general databases; selected library catalogues; organizations; and news sources. This email address is also of importance: *To receive current updates on U.S. Mexico border issues, send an email to mollymolloy@gmail.com.

Knight Center for Journalism in the Americas (http://knightcenter. utexas.edu): The Knight Center tracks issues related to journalism in the Americas. This site is especially valuable due to its coverage of impunity of cartel actions and attacks against journalists in Mexico and Latin America. In addition to a blog with current news and reports, it maintains a Twitter feed (@utknightcenter). See especially the Knight Center map of threats against Journalism at http://knightcenter.utexas.edu/blog/new-knight-center-map-pinpoints-threats-againstjournalism-mexico. A larger version of the Journalist Threat Map is found at Google maps: http://maps.google.com/maps/ms?ie=UTF8&hl=en&msa=0&msid=103960216204540664660.00048f4d72b6a3a226539&ll=24.327575,102.945411&spn=14.726415,12.091995&source=embed.

Los Angeles Times— Mexico Under Siege Series (http://projects.latimes.com/mexico-drugwar/#/its-a-war): *Since June 2008, *LA Times* reporters and photographers have chronicled, from both sides of the border, the savage struggle among Mexican drug cartels for control over the lucrative drug trade to the U.S. The conflict has left thousands dead, paralyzed whole cities with fear, and spawned a culture of corruption reaching the upper levels of the Mexican state. This extremely important site—one of the best covering this threat— provides a complete listing of dozens upon dozens of *LA Times* articles with topic and location filtering, an interactive map, multimedia gallery, and video Q&A by series editor Geoffrey Mohan. The site contains introductions to the topical area by David Shirk, Jorge Chabat, Sam Quinones, and others, user comments, and a Twitter feed (@mexicodrugwar) (this site is featured in this piece).

Mexican and Colombian Drug Cartels— FBI Library Subject Bibliography (http://fbilibrary.fbiacademy.edu/bibliographies/mexicanandcolombiandrugcartels.htm): This 2010 resource is an annotated listing of books, chapters, articles, and DVDs which provide information related to Mexican and Colombian Cartels. It was created for use by FBI National Academy students and others who utilize the FBI Library in Quantico, VA, by one of the authors of this piece.

Mexico Institute (http://www.mexicoinstitute.wordpress.com): The Mexico Institute is a specialty research program at the Woodrow Wilson International Center for Scholars. In addition to sponsoring research and publications—including the recent *Shared Responsibility U.S.-Mexico Policy Options for Confronting Organized Crime*, edited by Eric

L. Olson, David A. Shirk, and Andrew D. Selee—it maintains a current news site the Mexico Portal and a Twitter feed (@MexicoInstitute). See also the Mexico Portal at the site at http://www.wilsoncenter. org/index.cfm?fuseaction=topics.home&topic_id=5949. *The Mexico Portal provides comprehensive and timely news, analysis and studies on Mexico. It covers a wide range of crucial issues, including migration, security, the economy, development, energy, and elections.

Mexico's Drug War (http://borderviolenceanalysis.typepad.com/ mexicos_drug_war/): This small blog site is administered by *Sylvia [Longmire]...an independent consultant, author and freelance writer, and [who] contributes regularly to *Homeland Security Today* magazine and website. She is currently working on a book on Mexican cartels and how they've infiltrated America, which was picked up for publication by Palgrave Macmillan in Fall 2011. The administrator is a retired U.S. Air Force Captain with former experience as a Latin American desk officer. The site contains introductory level essays on the various cartels, resource links, social media feeds, archives, and category listings focused on *border incidents, border tunnels, commerce, corruption, current affairs, drug smuggling, DTOs, gangs, general violence, government and politics, human smuggling, in focus, kidnapping, terrorism, travel, and weapons trafficking.

MEXIDATA.INFO (http://www.mexidata.info/): Mexidata is a comprehensive Mexico area studies site. In addition to robust coverage of topical issues in Mexico's drug war, it contains links to current research, Mexican press reports, and current events. This is an excellent sit for gathering I&W and placing current events in context. The essays (original and reprints) are of a consistent high quality. The site also maintains a Twitter feed (@MexiData_info).

Narco Mexico (http://narcocartels.blogspot.com/): This omnibus site covers Mexican cartel and "narcocultura" events in English and Spanish. Good historical coverage, although updates are sporadic. Contains a glossary and blog entries that recap Mexican media reportage. A good first stop for English speakers seeking to gain a deeper understanding of events in Mexico. (Caveat: Needs updating, currently good for historical perspective).

The Narco News Bulletin (http://www.narconews.com/): This Progressive/ Left site covers narco violence and drug policy in Mexico and Latin America. It contains user/member generated content and is especially strong on contextual analysis. In addition to the blog it maintains a Twitter feed (@Narco_News). *Reportando sobre la guerra contra las drogas y la democracia desde América Latina* (Reporting on the Drug War and Democracy from Latin America).

Narcotrafico en Mexico (http://narcotraficoenmexico.blogspot.com/): This Spanish language blog provides current news updates and links to Mexican social media sites on narco issues. Similar to El Blog del Narco in content, it provides a valuable Twitter feed (@narcoenmexico). Good for current intel, context, and I&W; the Twitter feed is especially valuable. *Portal de noticias sobre el trafico de drogas* (News portal about drug trafficking). **En Español/Resource in Spanish.**

National Drug Intelligence Center (NDIC) (http://www.justice.gov/ ndic/): This U.S. governmental site is primarily useful for its links to drug war related publications. These publications include the National Drug Threat Assessment, National Gang Threat Assessment, and various Drug Assessments, Bulletins and Briefs, and Situation Reports. Information concerning Mexican cartels and gangs is highly authoritative yet typically outdated because of the long publication lag times involved. The publication *Cities in Which Mexican DTOs Operate Within the United States—Situation Report (2008)* is of immense importance for gaining an understanding of cartel geographic penetration into the United States. The site also provides information on SENTRY (A Synthetic Drug Early Warning and Response System) and the multiagency training course "Introduction to Basic Drug Intelligence Analysis".

Small Wars Journal—Roundup; Americas (http://smallwarsjournal.com/): Daily roundup provided by Dave Dilegge. Lists top news stories from *Associated Press, BBC News, Los Angeles Times, Reuters, Washington Post*, et. al., with many articles focusing on Mexican and Central American gang and cartel activity and violence and state response. This premier Small Wars site utilizes various social media plugins and Kindle updates. *Small Wars Journal* publishes contributed content from serious, authentic voices from across the wide spectrum of participants and stakeholders in small wars. *About: Small Wars Journal* facilitates the exchange of information among practitioners, thought leaders, and students of small wars, in order to advance knowledge and capabilities in the field. We hope this, in turn, advances the practice and effectiveness of those forces prosecuting Small Wars in the interest of self-determination, freedom, and prosperity for the population in the area of operations. *Small Wars Journal* is NOT a government, official, or big corporate site. It is run by Small Wars Foundation, a non profit corporation, for the benefit of the Small Wars community of interest. The site accepts donations and advertising with the foundation dating back to 2008. *Small Wars Journal* itself was launched in 2005.

Southern Pulse (http://www.southernpulse.com/): This site is administered by Samuel Logan (*This is for the Mara Salvatrucha; 2009*) and has been in existence since 2006. Useful pulses provided concerning gangs, cartels, and criminal activity in Latin America within the larger streams of information available. *Pulses are blocks of intelligence within the Southern Pulse network and database. Each pulse is a 2-5 sentence briefing of an internal piece of information, known as an Intel Feed. Pulses are intended to be direct and objective. The database contains pulses dating back to 2006 and can be searched with specific keywords. *Southern Pulse: Networked Intelligence is an information gathering and dissemination organization that uses field contacts and in country media sources to gather open source information on security, politics, energy, and business in Latin America. This fee service is $14.99 a month with access to over 3,800 pulses, field notes, briefs, and network query (human search engine) answering.

STRATFOR—Tracking Mexico's Drug Cartels (http://www.stratfor.com): Stratfor is a significant player in open source intelligence (OSINT). The Stratfor Mexico desk is a valuable resource for understanding the current and developing situation in Mexico's criminal insurgencies. Stratfor's analysts were among the first on the Mexican Drug War beat and regularly provide incisive analysis and projections about trends and potentials in the narco-conflict. Their *Mexico Security Memo* is an essential resource. While we don't always agree with their assessment, we would never miss it! Their products are essential reading. See especially http://www.strat for.com/theme/tracking_mexicos_drug_cartels.

Third Generation Gangs and Child Soldiers— FBI Library Subject Bibliography (http://fbilibrary.fbiacademy.edu/bibliographies/thirdgenerationgangs.htm): This 2007 resource is an annotated listing of books, chapters, articles, and DVDs which provide information related to Third Generation Gangs (politicized and military-like) and Child Soldiers. Such gangs and soldiers are found in the criminal insurgencies now taking place in Mexico and other regions of Latin America. It was created for use by FBI National Academy students and others who utilize the FBI Library in Quantico, VA, by the authors of this piece.

Trans-Border Institute (TBI) (http://www.sandiego.edu/peacestudies/tbi/): The TBI site belongs to what is becoming a premier university peace research institute, with one area of interest for *Small Wars* readers being that focused on Mexican security and justice issues. The Institute Director is David Shirk (away on Sabbatical) with Charles Pope currently serving as the Interim Director. *The Trans-Border Institute (TBI) was created in 1994 with two main objectives: 1) to promote border-related scholarship, activities, and community at the University of San Diego, and 2) to promote an active role for the University in the cross-border community. To realize these objectives, the Institute engages in a variety of programmatic activities and initiatives. The Institute is also soliciting donations to build up its endowment. The site provides information on current projects including: U.S.-Mexico Security Cooperation Project, USD-UABC Legal Education Program, Justice in Mexico Project (Crime Indicator Database), Mapping Project, and Border Interview Series. *To sign up to receive the free monthly Justice in Mexico news report, please contact justiceinmexico@sandiego.edu. Past projects are also listed along with briefs, funded research documents, publications, course information, photo gallery, research links, and blog listings. The site has numerous social media links.

The Washington Post—Mexico at War Series (http://www.washingtonpost.com/wpsrv/world/interactives/mexico-at-war/): *The Mexican government's war against powerful drug cartels has far-reaching ramifications for both Mexico and the United States. *Washington Post* correspondents working north and south of the U.S.-Mexico border are reporting on the impacts of the drug war in both countries. A report emailing function exists for this site, however, no social networking plugins were noted. The site contains articles, archive blog, videos, and photos going back to mid-2010, making it a less comprehensive resource than the more established *Los Angeles Times* site going back to mid-2008.

Conclusion

Mexico's Drug War— which we view as a set of interlocking criminal insurgencies — challenges Mexico and sovereignty in general. This post-modern conflict (criminal insurgency and crime wars are likely to be on the rise as a significant form of future war) is dynamic. As the conflict matures and spreads to other points (consider the now and future "Criminal Insurgencies in the Americas"[12]), on-going research, intelligence analysis, and policy assessment will be required. It is hoped that this resource set will assist in those analytical endeavors.

CHAPTER 13

THE MEXICAN CARTEL DEBATE: AS VIEWED THROUGH FIVE DIVERGENT FIELDS OF SECURITY STUDIES

Robert J. Bunker

Initially published February 11, 2011

THE MEXICAN CARTEL DEBATE is becoming increasingly more important to U.S. national security, however, it is also becoming ever more confused, heated, and at times downright nasty, with little agreement about what is taking place in Mexico or in other regions of the Americas, such as Guatemala, Honduras, and even this side of the U.S. border. To shed some light on this critical debate—a debate we need to have now and not later— it is the contention of this author that, since the Mexican cartel phenomena is being looked at by scholars from divergent fields of security studies and since each field of study brings with it its own key assumptions and concerns, preferred responses, terminology, works, and authors, those analyzing the problem are often talking at cross-purposes which is unproductive. Additionally, dissention among those within each individual field of study about the threat the cartels represent—the divergences among those who study insurgencies as but one important example— adds another layer of confusion to this debate.

    It can be argued that an ordinal threat continuum exists, differentiated by field of security study, of the danger that cartels represent to the

Mexican state and, in turn, those states bordering it. Taken together, these threat assessments are helping to actively influence U.S. public and governmental perceptions of the conflict now taking place in Mexico and, ultimately, help shape U.S. policy. While it is accepted that other major factors and biases are in play—U.S. federal and state governments and administrations, political parties and action committees, citizens groups, and the ideological leanings of the individual media outlets all attempt to influence this debate—academics and professionals aligned within recognized fields of security studies have a disproportionate impact due to their propensity to actively publish as well as get their messages out via other media. The debate benefits from each field's unique insights, unfortunately, these come with the baggage of having its own biases and their own interests at heart. Accordingly, some attempt will be made to mitigate the deleterious effects of this fact while seeking potential areas for cooperation between the fields.

Divergent Fields of Security Studies

Five primary fields of security studies are presently engaged, to one extent or another, in research and publication on the Mexican cartel phenomena and on the threat that this phenomena poses to that country, to the United States, and to other Western Hemispheric nations. Each field of security study will be summarized and its major assumptions, concerns, and authors highlighted:[1]

- *Gang Studies:* These studies fall primarily under the disciplines of sociology and criminal justice. Law enforcement practitioners in gang units, such as Wes McBride (Sgt. LASD, Ret), and university academics have long dominated this field. This field focuses on generic street and drug gangs, prison gangs, geographically focused (e.g. New York, Chicago, Los Angeles) gangs, specialized ethnic (e.g. Hispanic, African American) gangs and gender (female) gangs. Gangs with more organized structures—such as Asian and Outlaw Motorcycle— also fall into this field with some overlap into organized crime studies. The basic assumption is that street, drug, and prison gangs engage in "low intensity crime" activities and therefore they are a local law enforcement problem— though regional and national gang investigators associations have emerged for information sharing and coordination purposes due to the spread of these groups throughout the United States. Key authors in this field include the late Frederic Thrasher along with present day authors Malcolm Klein, George Knox, William Dunn, and John Hagedorn. [It must be noted that Hagedorn has recently rethought the usefulness of studies derived from traditional criminology—parting ways with the statement "De mortuis nil nisi bonum" (*Speak no ill of the dead*)[2]— and is branching out into terrorism and insurgency research due to the increasing global nature of armed young men and the growing influence of criminal networks.]

- *Organized Crime Studies:* This field, which covers both domestic and transnational (or global) organized crime, draws normally upon the disciplines of political science, history, and criminal justice. Organized criminal organizations and illicit economies are the center focus of these studies. It should be pointed out that the Mexican cartels are still drawing the bulk of their resources presently from illicit narcotics sales, but have also branched out into numerous other illicit endeavors including human trafficking, kidnapping, and street taxation. The basic assumption of this field is that organized crime entities seek to establish a parasitic (and symbiotic) relationship with their host state(s) and simply obtain freedom of actions for their illicit activities. Such criminal entities are viewed as solely money making endeavors, are not politicized, and have no intention of creating their own shadow political structures or taking over the reigns of governance. These studies view organized crime as the purview of law enforcement with specialized units (i.e. FBI and DEA task forces) required to dismantle the more sophisticated and dangerous criminal organizations. The conflict environment is said to be that of crime or organized crime with the extreme operational environment now found in Mexico being labeled as that of "high intensity crime". Key authors in this field include Phil Williams, Bruce Bagley, George Grayson, and Tony Rafael.

- *Terrorism Studies:* This field of studies emerged out of the late 1960s—as urban guerillas became politically motivated terrorists— with initial terrorism courses taught in the mid-to-late 1970s in political science and international relations departments. This field has had its assumptions shift from limited levels of violence utilized and the use of kidnappings as theater plays; hence "terrorists want lots of people watching— not dead"[3] to religiously motivated terrorists who seek to engage in killing on a mass scale. The basic assumption is that terrorists, both politically and religiously motivated, engage in destructive attacks that generate "terror" (a form of disruptive societal targeting) in order to change governmental policies. Further, terrorism is considered a technique that, when utilized in a revolutionary or insurgent setting, can help to create a shadow government and/or overthrow a government in power. Narco-terrorism would be considered a subfield of terrorism studies—though utilizing terror to promote criminal objectives. To date, many of the best and brightest terrorism scholars—except for Brian Jenkins who possesses insurgency expertise from the Vietnam era—have not made an attempt to engage in this area of research as it pertains to the cartels in Mexico. Depending on its severity and where it takes place, terrorism can be considered a law enforcement problem, a homeland security problem, and/or a military problem. Key authors in this field include Brian Jenkins, Stephen Sloan, Bruce Hoffman, David Rapoport, and Marc Sageman.

- *Insurgency Studies:* These studies are politico-military based and undertaken at think tanks, in some university departments, and at U.S. military and governmental institutions. They are the bread and butter focus of *Small Wars Journal* and get us into topical areas including revolutionary warfare, insurgency, guerrilla warfare, low intensity conflict, operations other than war, shadow governmental structures, and a host of other terms for this level of conflict and/or techniques. Since terrorism is also common as an insurgency technique, some bleed over from this field to terrorism studies exists as do some forays into organized crime studies, due to the benefits illicit economies provide to insurgents (for example, we might ask where the Taliban would be without its illicit narcotics income). This field predates Mao Zedong's works of the late 1930s and has been developing for over a half-century with key interest during the Vietnam era. The field is especially vibrant now with American involvement in Iraq and Afghanistan-Pakistan. Assumptions and concerns focus on political change and revolution, that is, how groups out of power in a country seize control of a government by indirect and irregular means not conventional military conquest. The latter may, however, be considered the final phase of revolutionary warfare so clearly the techniques used vary widely. Insurgency itself, if allowed to gain strength, is viewed as a national security threat to a state. This field of study is undergoing its own internal debate concerning the primacy of political based insurgency vs. broadening the definition of insurgency to include other forms derived from religion and/or criminality. The threat posed by the Mexican cartels encompasses this internal debate and raises the question as to whether Mexico is or is not facing "criminal insurgencies".[4] Key authors in this field include Max Manwaring, Graham Turbiville, Jr., T.X. Hammes, Steve Metz, and David Kilcullen.

- *Future Warfare Studies:* The areas of military and strategic studies, political science, international relations, and military history (via trend analysis) have all contributed to the study of future warfare. This form of study assumes that "modes of warfare" or "coherent warfare practices" exist and that warfare is continually evolving. Typically, this is attributed to the introduction of new forms of technology (such as the stirrup or gunpowder), an expansion of the battlespace into new temporal and spatial dimensions (such as the domain of cyberspace), or the rise of new military organizational forms (such as the legion or modern divisional structure). Multivariate explanations for the evolution of warfare also readily exist in this field of study. The threat represented by the Mexican cartels would therein be considered part of a modal warfare shift. This shift would, at a minimum, elevate the threat the Mexican cartels represent to that of a national security threat as the cartels would be engaging in a new form of warfare against the Mexican state—though a number of scholars would argue such a threat transcends national security and represents a threat to the nation-state form itself. Key authors in this field include Martin van Creveld, John Arquilla and David Ronfeldt, Phillip Bobbitt, John Robb, and the author of this essay along with his frequent collaborator and "intellectual wingman" John Sullivan.

- Numerous discipline and author omissions certainly exist concerning this security studies conceptual schema—country (Mexico) and area (Central and Latin America) and peace studies and conflict resolution scholars are not directly considered here. As a result, the important work of Roderic Camp (Mexican studies/army specialist), David Shirk (peace studies applied to Mexico), and Steven Dudley (Central America specialist), and the contributions of many others—including Ed Vulliamy, Hal Brands, Samuel Logan, Malcolm Beith, and David Danelo—would seemingly be overlooked. It is the perspective of this author, however, that their focuses and assumptions could and would be incorporated into this schema because they will weigh in on the Mexican cartel debate via their varying focuses as they fit within these five fields of security studies. Hypothetically, for instance, Roderic Camp might analyze the Mexican army at the level of organized crime studies—how effective is its policing operations—or just as easily analyze it at the terrorism or insurgency studies level and, as a result, measure how effective it is in either counter-terrorism or counter-insurgency operations.

Threat Continuum

The threat continuum represented by these five fields of security studies is ordinal in nature and begins at the micro level and extends to the macro level (Fig. 1).

**Figure 1. Threat Continuum with
Worst Case Scenarios for Mexico**

GANG STUDIES	*ORGANIZED CRIME STUDIES*	*TERRORISM STUDIES*	*INSURGENCY STUDIES*	*FUTURE WARFARE STUDIES*
Gangs take control of neighborhoods, prisons, and drug markets	Cartel creation of 'zones of impunity' to freely engage in illicit economic pursuits (no political agendas)	Cartel use of narco-terrorism to obtain Mexican governmental concessions (to benefit criminal activities)	Indirect cartel take over/ alliance with Mexican government via a parallel shadow government (politicized cartels)	Rise of a new warmaking entity (criminal & networked) that controls territories, population centers, and sovereign governments

As applied to Mexico, each field envisions a "worst case scenario" that characterizes the severity of the threat as it is derived from the parameters of that field of study. These worst case scenarios and governmental threat perceptions, theoretical insights, and other important developments are as follows:

Gang Members/Street & Prison Gangs: The worst case scenario at this level of threat is for gangs to control neighborhoods and prisons or drug markets in different sections of cities or towns. **Operational environments: crime and low intensity crime.**

Virtually no one thinks the threat to Mexico exists solely at this level, although these groups are integral allies and/or contractors to the cartels for intelligence, security, drug distribution, and enforcement services. From the perspective of 3GEN Gangs theory, these groups represent 1st (Turf) and 2nd (Drug) gangs. Increasingly, law enforcement agencies from Los Angeles and other U.S. cities are providing gang unit support to Mexico and Central American countries concerning this threat.

Drug Dealers and Enforcers/Drug Trafficking Organizations: The worst case scenario is DTOs (or cartels) creating "zones of impunity" which provide them with the ability to engage in their activities without governmental hindrance. These organizations simply seek to make money via illicit means and have no desire to be involved in politics or governance. Corruption is utilized, along with violence, to obtain freedom of action for their criminal activities. **Operational environments: crime, organized crime, and high intensity crime.**

The Calderon administration has stated that this level accurately reflects the security threat facing Mexico. The Mexican cartels are said to represent the forces of organized crime and nothing more, even though some hundreds of "zones of impunity" are recognized to exist and the deployment of military forces to maintain civil order in some of the cities in Mexico continues. The DEA and FBI are heavily involved in suppressing the various Mexican cartels in the United States (e.g. Operation Deliverance, Operation Xcellerator, Project Coronado) and insuring that the corruption coming over the border does not deeply penetrate our public law enforcement agencies (e.g. FBI-led Border Corruption Task Forces are expanding). These and other U.S. Federal Law Enforcement Agencies are also active in Mexico and Central America in responding to Mexican drug trafficking organization activities.

Terrorists/Terrorist Groups: The worst case scenario for this level of threat is cartel use of narco-terrorist tactics—bombings and standup assaults, kidnappings, and other forms of violence directed at the Mexican public (e.g. the grenade attacks in Morelia, Michoacán, in September 2008)— to obtain political concessions from the Mexican federal government so that the cartels can freely continue with their illicit activities. Cartel weapons of mass destruction (WMD) use potentials have never been contemplated and this threat is viewed to exist at the "gun and the bomb" level only. **Operational environments: terrorism and homeland security.**

Terrorist tactics are actually being used against other cartels (to eliminate or scare off organized crime competitors/secure illicit revenues), against Mexican police and military forces (in a classic insurgency role), and at times against the Mexican public (as a form of narco-terrorism). Both Federal Mexican law enforcement and the Mexican military are being forced to develop counter-terrorism and force protection capabilities to respond to the use of terrorism. Of interest is the January 2011 suggestion by Edgardo Buscaglia, a fellow at the Autonomous Technological Institute of Mexico (ITAM), that Los Zetas and other cartel groups be designated as terrorists under U.N. statutes. This suggestion, however, will go nowhere with the Calderon administration. From the perspective of the U.S. State Department, it may hold some eventual merit since the Revolutionary Armed Forces of Colombia (FARC) and the United Self-Defense Forces of Colombia (AUC)—Colombian insurgents involved in drug trafficking— are so designated under its Foreign Terrorist Organizations (FTOs) designations.

Insurgents/Insurgent Groups: The worst case scenario is an indirect cartel (criminal) takeover of the Mexican government and/or alliance with it by means of the creation of a parallel shadow government. This would imply the installation of a new Mexican president and ruling party controlled by, most likely, the Sinaloa Cartel, representing a multi-cartel and multi-gang coalition. Numerous shadow governments at the city and town (and possibly even state governor) levels already exist in Mexico. This would be an extension of the process of the assassination of local mayors, suppression of the free press, and mass corruption of many public officials already taking place. **Operational environments: small wars, insurgency, low intensity conflict, and guerilla warfare.**

The Obama Administration in September 2010, via Secretary of State Hillary Clinton, injected a "trial balloon" in the Mexican cartel debate. The conflict in Mexico was said to be beginning to appear like the insurgencies that have taken place in Colombia. This was immediately met with a strong diplomatic rebuke by the Calderon administration and resulted in President Obama personally apologizing for the comparison. Absolutely no mention was made of the threat embodied by the Mexican cartels during Obama's January 2011 State of the Union address, suggesting that this issue, compounded by the released Wikileaks diplomatic messages, has made any public statements concerning this threat too politically sensitive to be issued. In February 2011, Undersecretary of the Army Joseph Westphal speaking at a public forum at a University in Utah said "As all of you know, there is a form of insurgency in Mexico with the drug cartels that's right on our border...This is about, potentially, a takeover of a government by individuals who are corrupt."[6] These words received a fierce rebuke by the Calderon administration that resulted in Undersecretary Westphal quickly apologizing and withdrawing his public statement. At the same time that the "I" word has been mentioned in the public media and shot down by the Calderon administration, the U.S. has been quietly providing counter-insurgency aid and training to Mexican military forces.

Non–State (Criminal) Soldiers/Criminal Armies: Threats at this level basically represent criminal challengers to the nation-state form that are extremely hostile to traditional states such as Mexico and the United States. The worst case scenario is that of the rise of a new warmaking entity—one that is network organized—establishing itself in Mexico and other nations of the Americas and, as it grows in strength, takes control of transnational territories and population centers including that of sovereign governments. Al Qaeda, by the way, would be considered representative of another one of these new and still evolving warmaking entities. **Operational environments: the blurring of crime and war, hybrid war, netwar, post-modern war.**

Such a worst case scenario is usually found only in scholarly books and papers, which rarely get much attention or readership outside the field, and in governmental and military analytical products on future threats, typically not for public disclosure. This author can only speak to the former of these worst case scenarios. Martin van Creveld's *The Transformation of War* (1991) is the best known work in this regard, especially when we remember his prophetic statement—"In the future, war will not be waged by armies but by groups whom we today call terrorists, guerrillas, bandits and robbers, but who will undoubtedly hit on more formal titles to describe themselves" (p. 197). A sole focus on his work alone would take us deep into debates on the merits and detractions of non-trinitarian warfare, therefore, it must be realized that extensive work has been done in this area of security studies by many other authors. Terms associated with this level of threat include 3GEN (politicized/mercenary) Gangs, 3rd Phase Cartels, Epochal Change, BLACKFOR, Revolution in Political and Military Affairs (RPMA), and "Criminal Insurgencies" as a component of an RPMA which takes place during periods of Epochal Change. Of interest is Guatemalan President Alvaro Colom's "remarkable call for a unified counternarcotics force that would set aside nationalist rivalries to combine soldiers from Guatemala, El Salvador and Honduras to retake territory from the expanding crime syndicates" in January 2011.[7] For Guatemala, which has imposed a "state of siege" and martial law in Alta Verapaz province due to Los Zetas and Sinaloan cartel invasions, the threat represented by criminal-armies has become a reality.

It would be fair to say that attributes of the Mexican cartels and their network affiliates exist all along this threat continuum from the micro to the macro level of concern. Hence, all of these fields of security studies should rightfully be involved in analyzing this complex threat to the Mexican state. It should also be noted that much of the violence taking place in Mexico is cartel network vs. cartel network —these entities and their gang and mercenary allies are fighting over lucrative drug plazas and transit routes, new illicit revenue opportunities, influence and control over Mexican public officials, and even petty squabbles over perceived slights to one's honor. This is truly making the conflict taking place in Mexico resemble a free-for-all with ever shifting cartel and gang alliances and even different Mexican governmental institutions and public officials either siding with, or in actuality members of, one cartel or another.

Stove Pipes, Rice Bowls, and Areas of Cooperation

The problem of the narrow compartmentalization of fields (i.e. stove pipes) and the fight for a part of limited resources (i.e. rice bowls) as it pertains to debating the threat posed by the Mexican cartels, before one even gets to the problem of responding to the violence and corruption carried out by these cartels and their affiliates, is nothing new. It was discussed by this author in the earlier *Narcos Over the Border* work as it pertained to the seven trans-operational environments involving U.S. engagement with Mexican cartels, mercenaries and Sureños gangs in the Americas.[8]

Each discipline represents a cohesive area of study with its own level of concern and focus of threat emphasis. For simple threats, such as a specific street gang— like the Hicks gang in El Monte, California— the gang studies (in the applied sense, gang suppression) approach utilized by local law enforcement is adequate for the task at hand. The same could be said for organized crime studies and the New York based mafias—scholars within the field are able to successfully analyze them and FBI lead task forces are well suited to contend with such threats.

These traditional organizational structures—combining scholars and more applied professionals (e.g. gang cops, FBI agents, and intelligence analysts)—as an extension of the differing fields of security studies begin to falter, however, when faced with more complex threats. In this instance, the extreme specialization that works so well for focusing on a specific threat—be it gangs, organized criminals, terrorists or insurgents— can become a great liability. Members belonging to these divergent security fields hold very different viewpoints about what constitutes a threat, which threats are more important than others, and how they should be addressed, and may even possess extremely different professional cultures. Sometimes these security fields, especially within much larger agencies or between academic departments and think tank divisions, come into conflict when they compete for finite resources to engage in their activities. Ultimately, this extreme specialization means that wide "informational seams" exist between insular, and at times competing, fields of security studies. An attempt to get two or more of these fields together to contend with a complex threat such as that posed by the Mexican cartels (and their vast network of gang and mercenary auxiliaries) likely means that major problems will ensue. These problems multiply as more fields are required to contend with a complex threat. If personnel representing fields at opposite ends of the threat continuum are brought together to work on a threat issue—assuming you can get such differing security professionals together in the first place—then the problems may multiply exponentially.

What is clear is that complex post-modern threats—such as those posed by the Mexican cartels and, for that matter, Al Qaeda and its affiliate network— do not fit into neat categories and well-defined security fields. What is needed is for a U.S. governmental "honest broker" or supra-security organization to come into the Mexican cartel debate and leverage the five fields of security studies highlighted in this essay into a broader networked effort. This effort must further be tied into issues pertaining to the trans-operational environments involving U.S. engagement with Mexican cartels and their affiliates. We can no longer afford the luxury of watching numerous fields of study and security response organizations—each with their own form of "extreme specialization"— independently going about their activities in a totally uncoordinated manner. Instead, attention should be directed at creating a hemispheric strategy for the Americas, possibly even global in scale, to directly challenge the rise of the Mexican cartels and their mercenary and gang affiliates along the entire threat continuum highlighted in this essay.

CHAPTER 14

ATTACKS ON JOURNALISTS AND "NEW MEDIA" IN MEXICO'S DRUG WAR: A POWER AND COUNTER POWER ASSESSMENT

John P. Sullivan
Initially published April 9, 2011

THIS PAPER EXAMINES THE impact of attacks on journalists on media reportage within Mexico's drug wars, known as "la Inseguridad" in Mexico. It examines two concepts in communication theory (agenda-setting theory and "mind framing" for power and counter-power) to frame the impact of drug cartel information operations (info ops).[1] Specifically, It examines cartel attacks on media outlets, and kidnappings and assassinations of journalists by narco-cartels to gauge the potential impact of the attacks in terms of censorship, cartel co-option of reportage, and the use of new media (horizontal means of mass self-communication).

Introduction

MEXICO IS IN THE midst of a significant conflict between drug cartels and the state. This war for control of illicit economic space (transnational drug trafficking and the criminal economy) is also a battle for legitimacy, turf, and power. As part of this contest for control of the *plazas* (drug transshipment nodes), cartels and gangs are seeking to remove the control or interference of the state so they can freely operate. Since 2006 when President Calderón declared war on the cartels, over 28,000-30,000 persons2 have been killed in the brutal drug wars (Trans-Border Institute, 2010).

An increasingly significant component of this violence has been directed against journalists and media outlets in an effort to silence the media so the cartels can operate with impunity. Television stations (such as Televisa in Tamaulipas and Nuevo León) have been attacked with grenades, journalists assassinated, kidnapped or disappeared. According to the Committee to Protect Journalists (2010), at least 30 journalists have been killed or disappeared in Mexico in the past four years, and 11 have been killed in 2010 alone. A detailed map tracking violence against Mexican journalists has been developed by The Knight Center for Journalism in the Americas at the University of Texas, Austin (Knight Center, 2010).

Communications Theory and Narco-conflict

Agenda-setting theory (McCombs and Shaw, 1972) postulates that the media influences audiences through their choice of coverage. This is widely described as "salience transfer" where the media transfers its agenda to the public through the media's emphasis of various issues. In this framework, media, public, policy, and corporate agendas are determined in part through media reportage. As we will see, cartel info ops negate (or at least severely challenge) the media's agenda setting capacity.

Communication power and counter-power are key components of the evolution of the network society (Castells, 2007). The media has become the social space where power is decided. As a consequence, politics, media politics, and political legitimacy are at stake in the global competition for power in the network society. Indeed, communication and information are now fundamental sources of power and counter-power, domination and social change.

Power is the structural capacity of a social actor to impose its will over other social actors. The state, traditionally a main locus of power, is being challenged globally by a number of factors, including globalization, market forces, and crises of legitimacy. Mexico's drug war is a salient example of the challenges faced by states from one variety of globalization: transnational organized crime. Mind framing is the process through which power is exercised. In the Mexican situation,

I believe we will see evidence that cartels are exerting raw power (symbolic and instrumental violence) as part of their efforts to shape their operating environment(s). Cartel power-making includes mind framing, and by influencing or censoring media reportage, cartels are shaping the media space where power is decided.

> New media is an emerging component of this battle for ideas, the power-counter-power contest. A range of actors (*i.e.,* the media, citizens, bloggers, and cartels) are reportedly appropriating new forms of communication (blogs, wikis, micro-blogs, etc.) to navigate the cartel wars. As a result, the rise of "mass self-communication" is an integral element of the drug war and has the potential of becoming an important medium of transmitting information and shaping the outcome of the conflict. The concept of "counter-power" or the capacity of social actors to challenge and eventually change institutionalized power relations is a critical component of understanding the cartels' information operations. As Castells (2007) observed, "The emergence of mass self-communication offers an extraordinary medium for social movements and rebellious individuals to build their autonomy and confront the institutions of society in their own terms and around their own projects." For the drug cartels, this means to control the *plazas* for the trans-shipment of drugs, limit competition from other cartels, and eliminate interference from the state.

The Drug War: Mexico's "Criminal Insurgencies"

Mexico's criminal gangs and drug trafficking organizations (cartels) are expanding their reach and power. They are essentially engaged in a protracted war against each other and the state. Since 1996, when the Government of Mexico declared war on the cartels, between 28,000–30,000 persons have been killed in the cartels' quest to dominate lucrative global narco-markets.

The cartels are fighting at three levels: within their own enterprises for dominance, against other cartel alliances, and against the security forces of the state (police and military) to fend off interference. This in my view amounts to a series of interlocking "criminal insurgencies" (Sullivan & Elkus, 2010) and an effort by the cartels to secure a form of "dual sovereignty" (Grayson, 2010) where the cartels can operate without interference and with impunity.

At least eight cartels (and a number of smaller affiliated gangs) are engaged in this battle for dominance of Mexico's criminal economy. The major players include Los Zetas, the Sinaloa cartel, the Gulf cartel, the Juárez cartel, the Tijuana cartel, the Beltran-Leyva Organization, and La Familia Michoacana. Influence operations and shaping communication through violence and attacks on journalists are becoming an important element in support of their economic strategy and emerging political goals.

Censoring the News

It is widely reported that cartels are conducting information operations to further their campaign to dominate Mexico's illicit economy. For example, in a recent essay "Analysis: A PR department for Mexico's narcos" at *GlobalPost*, Mike O'Connor notes that newspapers in Ciudad Victoria, Tamaulipas are running press releases for the Zetas. This development, occurring in the midst of a battle for supremacy among the Los Zetas and their former allies the Cartel del Golfo (Gulf Cartel), seeks to shape public perception and intimidate adversaries.

Essentially, it is a battle for legitimacy—to determine who rules. Zetas promote stories of military human rights abuses to turn the public against Federal intervention and stories about police prowess to support co-opted police allied to their cartel. As O'Connor noted, "Cartel control is growing across Mexico, and the press is often one of the cartels' first targets. Their objective is to keep the public ignorant of their actions." This paper seeks to frame this situation with theory and empirical observations.

Assault on the Press: Assassinations, Kidnappings and Attacks

On 18 September 2010, *El Diario*, Ciudad Juarez's newspaper (currently edited across the international frontier in El Paso) printed an unprecedented editorial *¿Qué quieren de nosotros?* In English, simply "What do you want from us?" Published the day after one of its photographers was murdered, the editorial provides a stark illustration of the intense assault against Mexico's free press by cartel gangsterism. The *El Diario* editorial (translation at *Los Angeles Times, La Plaza*) read in part:

Gentlemen of the different organizations that are fighting for the Ciudad Juarez plaza, the loss of two reporters of this news organization represents an irreparable breakdown for all of us who work here, and in particular, for our families.

We'd like you to know that we're communicators, not psychics. As such, as information workers, we ask that you explain what it is you want from us, what you'd intend for us to publish or to not publish, so that we know what is expected of us.

You are at this time the *de facto* authorities in this city because the legal authorities have not been able to stop our colleagues from falling, despite the fact that we've repeatedly demanded it from them. Because of this, before this undeniable reality, we direct ourselves to you with these questions, because the last thing we want is that another one of our colleagues falls victim to your bullets.

Attacks against journalists in Mexico have been rising throughout the drug war and the consensus in the media and among journalists is that it has reached a critical mass. As a result Reporters Sans Frontiéres characterizes press freedom in Mexico as being in a "difficult situation" (see Figure One) for 2011.

Figure One: Press Freedom Nations at Risk, 2011

Source: Reporters Sans Frontiéres

Indeed, the two leading press freedom indices (Freedom House Freedom of Press Index and Reporters Sans Frontiéres Press Freedom Index) have been deteriorating since the start of Mexico's Drug War in 2006 (see Table One). The Freedom House index gives Mexico a score of 60 (partially free) for 2010. That score is on the cusp of being rated "not free"(a score of 61-100). In 2005 the year before the current "inseguridad" began, the score was 42. Similarly, the Freedom House index has deteriorated each year from 45.50 in 2005 to 48.25 in 2009 (where 0 is perfect).

Table One: Press Freedom Indices: 2005-2010

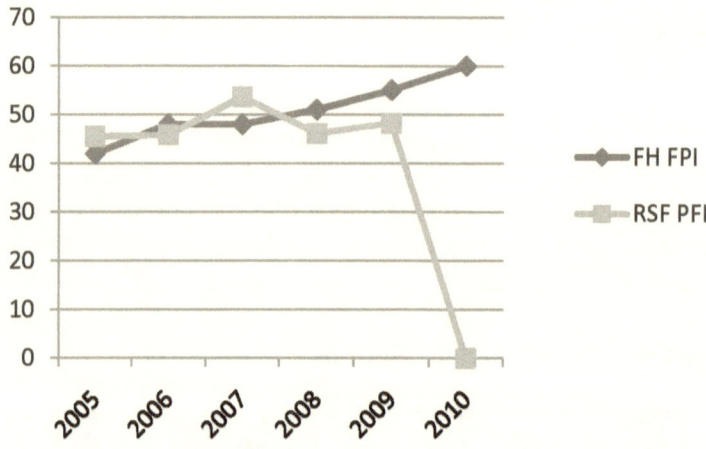

Source: Freedom House and Reporters Sans Frontiéres

In its report "Silence or Death in Mexico's Press," the Committee to Protect Journalists (CPJ) (2010) suggested that attacks on journalists are not simply a matter of cartels suppressing some damaging stories, rather "Their motives are much more complicated and sinister." According to the CPJ, cartels suppress stories about their own violence while paying journalists to play up the savagery of their rivals and damage competing operations by planting stories about corrupt officials. The CPJ observes that competing cartels throughout Mexico have developed aggressive media tactics as a component for their battles for the *plazas*. As a result, "The traffickers rely on media outlets they control to discredit their rivals, expose corrupt officials working for competing cartels, defend themselves against government allegations, and influence public opinion."

Consequently, "Competing criminal organizations are controlling the information agenda in many cities across Mexico" (CPJ, 2010, p. 2). Violence is one means of gaining this control. According to CPJ, 22 journalists have been murdered since December 2006, at least eight in direct reprisal for reporting crime and corruption. In addition, three media support workers have been slain and at least seven journalists have gone missing (potentially "disappeared"), while dozens of other have been attacked, kidnapped, or forced into exile. The impact of this operation seems concentrated in specific contested areas. For example, "In Reynosa, the Gulf criminal group controls the government, the police, even the street vendors. You won't see that story in the local press. The cartel controls the media, too" (CPJ, 2010. p. 15).

As a result, Mexican journalists are facing a serious emergency and threat to their safety and profession. According to the Knight Center's report *Journalism in Times of Threats, Censorship and Violence* (Medel, 2010) a cartel news blackout in Reynosa in March 2010 involved a cartel blockade on entry of foreign journalists into the contested region. In August 2010, four reporters in La Laguna were kidnapped (Medel, 2010). According to the Knight Center: "Mexico is going through a phase of open warfare and shifting alliances among seven or eight large criminal groups (and many small ones) that each have a capacity for damage and corruption." For the media, this means, "The *narcos* impose totalitarian regimes on local communities under their control, and freedom of the press is their first victim. Mexico is home to dozens of "zones of silence"—and in some cases, entire regions—where, if news is published it is only if "spokespersons" designated by the narcos gather journalists, authorize what to say and what to censor, and dictate to editors by phone even how to frame photographs in their newspapers" (Medel, 2010).

Assessing News Blackouts

News blackouts have become a feature of the Mexican drug war. This has two facets: government information operations and cartel info ops. According to the Knight Center, "coverage of drug trafficking in Mexico has been based generally on an official view of the facts… Releasing information a bit at a time allows Mexico's government to construct a public image of winning the war" (Medel, 2010, p. 22). Coupled with cartel efforts to obscure their hand through instrumental attacks and threats against journalists, the resulting pressure has resulted in near complete media blackouts in some areas.

The Foundación MEPI (*Foundación Mexican de Periodismo de Investigación*) recently completed a six-month study of 11 regional newspapers in Mexico to gauge the impact of cartel interference or influence on reportage of cartel crime. The Fd. MEPI study relied on content analysis of the papers coverage and interviews with journalists. The report found that the regional newspapers were failing to report many cartel/narco crimes. In order to conduct the study, Fd. MEPI constructed a list of execution-style murders tied to cartel actions and then compared it to regional coverage. In all regions, the number of stories mentioning cartel violence from January to June 2010 amounted to a small fraction of the actual incidents. Consider for example that cartel murders in Cd. Juárez averaged an estimated 300 per month in 2010, but during the study period *El Norte*, the regional paper mentioned less than 10% or 30 per month. The impact appears even greater in eastern Mexico, where *El Mañana* in Nuevo Laredo published only 3 stories out of a potential 98 in June. Areas controlled by the Gulf and Zeta (*e.g.*, Taumalipas) cartels appear particularly impacted by the cartel blackout effect with between 0-5% of cartel violence stories reported. (Drug killings in Mexico by State for the same time period are displayed in Table Two.)

Table Two: "Drug Killings" in Mexico: January-June 2010

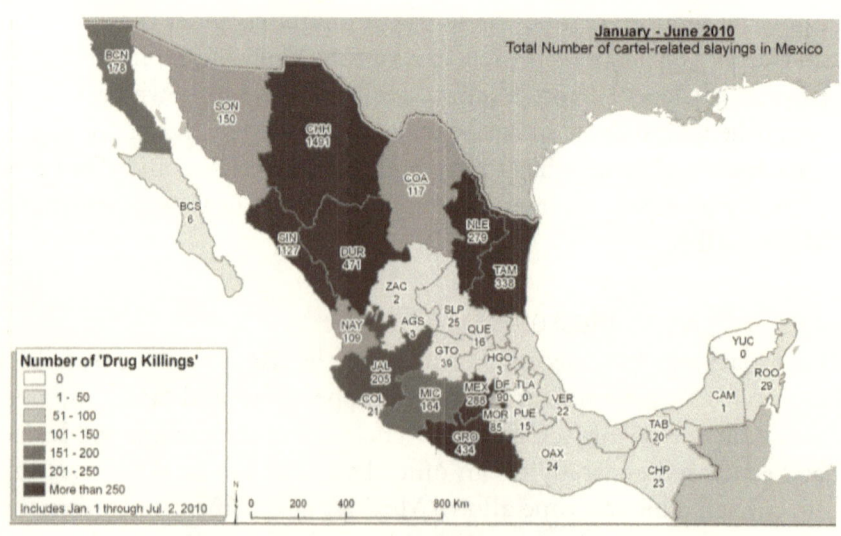

Source: Trans-Border Institute, University of San Diego

The Fd. MEPI analysis is presented in Table Three. Specifically, it reviewed the crime stories published in January-June 2010 from the following newspapers: *El Noroeste* (Culiacán), *El Norte* (Cd. Juárez), *El Dictamen* (Veracruz), *Mural* (Guadalahara), *Pulso* (San Luis Potosi), *El Mañana* (Nuevo Laredo), *El Diario de Morelos* (Morelos), *El Imparcial* (Hermosillo), *La Voz de Michoacán* (Morelia) and *Milenio* (Hidalgo). In 8 of the 13 cities studied, the papers reported only one of every ten narco violence stories; in the cities with more reportage, only 3 out of 10 were published.

Table Three: MEPI Analysis of Cartel News Blackouts: January-June 2010.

Table Three: MEPI Analysis of Cartel News Blackouts: January-June 2010.

Stories Published by Provincial Media on Drug trafficking compared to Gangland Slayings

NUEVO LEÓN (EL NORTE)

	Police stories that do not mention drug trafficking	Police stories that do mention drug trafficking	Gangland Executions	Police stories that mention executions
January	262	16	44	2
February	236	14	42	5
March	219	34	81	9
April	245	29	52	11
May	238	40	118	9
June	254	13	41	7

Morelia (La Voz de Michoacán)

	Police stories that do not mention drug trafficking	Police stories that do mention drug trafficking	Gangland Executions	Police stories that mention executions
January	198	21	67	5
February	173	17	41	4
March	210	22	68	1
April	183	21	60	4
May	179	14	65	0
June	187	11	61	3

HIDALGO (MILENIO)

	Police stories that do not mention drug trafficking	Police stories that do mention drug trafficking	Gangland Executions	Police stories that mention executions
January	45	6	19	2
February	34	7	9	0
March	64	6	12	0
April	50	11	12	2
May	49	9	12	4
June	58	4	6	1

CULIACÁN (EL NOROESTE)

	Police stories that do not mention drug trafficking	Police stories that do mention drug trafficking	Gangland Executions	Police stories that mention executions
January	48	16	27	12
February	63	16	23	8
March	70	19	29	8
April	133	46	29	32
May	169	48	21	33
June	190	23	11	20

MORELOS (EL DIARIO DE MORELOS)

	Police stories that do not mention drug trafficking	Police stories that do mention drug trafficking	Gangland Executions	Police stories that mention executions
January	30	6	10	5
February	34	4	9	3
March	21	14	15	8
April	17	21	9	14
May	16	15	8	8
June	41	34	6	14

VERACRUZ (EL DICTAMEN DE VERACRUZ)

	Police stories that do not mention drug trafficking	Police stories that do mention drug trafficking	Gangland Executions	Police stories that mention executions
January	39	9	11	0
February	33		23	3
March	38	1	26	2
April	52	3	27	1
May	56	2	39	1
June	70	4	28	2

C.D JUÁREZ (NORTE DIGITAL)

	Police stories that do not mention drug trafficking	Police stories that do mention drug trafficking	Gangland Executions	Police stories that mention executions
January	n/a	n/a	280	0
February	58	16	226	21
March	47	23	299	28
April	40	15	248	22
May	60	27	329	31
June	36	38	260	28

SONORA (EL IMPARCIAL)

	Police stories that do not mention drug trafficking	Police stories that do mention drug trafficking	Gangland Executions	Police stories that mention executions
January	38	38	53	12
February	48	37	36	15
March	55	30	34	14
April	72	35	35	8
May	46	37	34	11
June	50	24	21	9

SAN LUIS POTOSÍ (PULSO)

	Police stories that do not mention drug trafficking	Police stories that do mention drug trafficking	Gangland Executions	Police stories that mention executions
January	95	0	2	0
February	285	1	4	1
March	323	0	5	0
April	291	0	4	0
May	348	2	6	0
June	296	1	4	0

GUADALAJARA (MURAL)

	Police stories that do not mention drug trafficking	Police stories that do mention drug trafficking	Gangland Executions	Police stories that mention executions
January	179		11	5
February	156	10	24	0
March	210	18	26	5
April	209	20	27	6
May	193	14	39	0
June	193	25	28	5

NUEVO LAREDO (EL MAÑANA)

	Police stories that do not mention drug trafficking	Police stories that do mention drug trafficking	Gangland Executions	Police stories that mention executions
January	259	5	2	0
February	n/a	n/a	41	0
March	271	5	83	0
April	268	0	81	0
May	288	2	59	0
June	276	3	98	0

Source: Fundación MEPI; http://fundacionmepi.org/media/img/ investigacion1/tablas.jpg

Out of concern over the situation facing journalists in Mexico, the Knight Center for Journalism in the Americas developed a Google map tracking attacks against journalists (Knight Center, 2010). Thus far this year the map tracked 24 incidents (including 10 murders, 5 kidnapping incidents-including multiple victims in some cases, and 9 other type attacks). A comparison of Fd. MEPI reports of gangland executions and Knight Center incidents tracked between January-June 2010 is contained in Table Four.

Table Four: Stories Mentioning Gangland Executions Compared to Attacks on Journalists by Type, January-June 2010

City/State (Paper)	Stories Mentioning Gangland Executions	Journalists Killed	Journalists Kidnapped	Other Attacks on Journalists
Monterrey/ Nuevo León (*El Norte*)	43	1	0	1
Pachuca/ Hidalgo (*Milenio*)	9	0	0	0
Cuerneva/ Morales (*El Diario de Morelos*)	52	0	0	0
Ciudad Juárez/ Chihuahua (*Norte Digital*)	128	0	0	0
San Luis Potosi/San Luis Potosi (*Pulso*)	1	0	0	0
Nuevo Laredo/ Tamaulipas (*El Mañana*)	0	0	8	0
Morelia/ Michoacán (*La Voz de Michoacán*)	17	5	1	0
Culiacán/ Sinaloa (*El Noroeste*)	113	1	0	2

Xalapa/ Veracruz (*El Dictamen de Veracruz*)	9	0	1	0
Hermosillo/ Sonora (*El Imparcial*)	69	0	0	0
Guadalajara/ Jalisco (*Mural*)	21	0	0	0

Source: Knight Center and Fd. MEPI

Specifically, attacks on journalists were found at *El Norte* in Monterrey (Nuevo León), *El Mañana* in Nuevo Laredo (Tamaulipas), *La Voz de Michoacán* in Morelia (Michoacán), *El Noroeste* in Culicán (Sinaloa), and *El Dictaman de Veracruz* in Xalapa (Veracruz).

The impact of reportage at the 11 papers studied is depicted in Table Five.

Table Five: Change in Violence and Coverage by paper, January-June 2010

City/State (Paper)	Violence	Coverage
Monterrey/ Nuevo León (*El Norte*)	⇧ Increased	⇩ Decreased
Pachuca/ Hidalgo (*Milenio*)	⇧ Increased	⇩ Decreased
Cuerneva/ Morales (*El Diario de Morelos*)	⇧ Increased	⇧ Increased
Ciudad Juárez/ Chihuahua (*Norte Digital*)	⇧ Increased	⇧ Increased
San Luis Potosi / San Luis Potosi (*Pulso*)	⇧ Increased	= Same

Nuevo Laredo/ Tamaulipas (*El Mañana*)	⇧ Increased	⇩ Decreased
M o r e l i a / Michoacán (*La Voz de Michoacán*)	⇧ Increased	⇩ Decreased
Culiacán/ Sinaloa (*El Noroeste*)	⇩ Decreased	⇩ Decreased
Xalapa/ Veracruz (*El Dictamen de Veracruz*)	⇧ Increased	⇧ Increased
Hermosillo/ Sonora (*El Imparcial*)	⇧ Increased	⇧ Increased
G u a d a l a j a r a / Jalisco (*Mura*l)	⇧ Increased	⇩ Decreased

Source: Fd. MEPI

The specific results at the papers that experienced attacks is as follows:

El Norte: Monterrey, Nuevo León experienced a rise in violence and a decrease in coverage. Nuevo León has seen an increase in narco-executions from 217 in the first half of 2009 to 552 during the first half of 2010. Los Zetas and the Gulf cartel both operate in the state and are engaged in a bloody contest for control of the territory. Local reporters no longer use individual bylines. During the study period 43 stories mentioned gangland executions; one journalist was killed, and journalists were subjected to one other attack.

El Mañana: **Nuevo Laredo, Tamaulipas** experienced a rise in violence and a decrease in coverage. During the first half of 2010 it experienced a major rise in executions: 379 in January-June 2010 versus 49 in all of 2009. The area is considered a Gulf cartel stronghold. The paper's editor was killed outside his home in 2004 and in 2006 two hooded gunmen attacked the newsroom paralyzing a reporter. The paper admits self-censorship after these attacks. It ran no stories about gangland executions during the study period and eight journalists were kidnapped in the state during the study period.

La Voz de Michoacán: Morelia, Michoacán experienced a rise in violence and a decrease in coverage. During the first half of 2010 executions rose significantly to 1,605, up from 220 in 2009. The area was involved in a ballet between La Familia and the Milenio cartel. Two staff members of the paper were killed between April and July of 2010 both following cartel threats. The paper ran 17 stories about gangland executions, during the study period. Five journalists were killed and one kidnapped in the state during the same period.

La Voz de Michoacán: **Morelia, Michoacán** experienced a rise in violence and a decrease in coverage. During the first half of 2010 executions rose significantly to 1,605, up from 220 in 2009. The area was involved in a ballet between La Familia and the Milenio cartel. Two staff members of the paper were killed between April and July of 2010 both following cartel threats. The paper ran 17 stories about gangland executions, during the study period. Five journalists were killed and one kidnapped in the state during the same period.

El Dictamen: Xalapa, Veracruz experienced a rise in violence and a decrease in coverage during the first six months of 2010. The state also experienced a significant rise in executions during the first six months of this year with 45 incidents compared to 55 for all of 2009. The Zetas are believed to exercise complete control over the region. During the study period nine stories on gangland executions were printed and one journalist was kidnapped in the state. In 2008, 96 complaints of attacks against journalists were filed with state authorities.

These papers' experiences appear to be illustrative of the crisis in Mexican journalism in the face of the drug war. After the study period (January to June 2010) the assault against journalists and the media continued. According to the IAPA (Inter American Press Association) armed men attacked the Televisa facility in Torreón with AR-15 rifles; in July four journalists were kidnapped after covering a prison mutiny in Durango; in September the Mazatlán newspaper *Noroeste* was victim of a drive-by shooting. In October *El Debate* in Mazatlán was attacked with assault weapon fire. IAPA notes that seven journalists were murdered between May and

November 2010. In total, 65 journalists have been reported murdered in Mexico since 2005, 12 are suspected "disappeared" and 16 news media buildings have been attacked (IAPA, 2010).

Information Operations and Attacks on Journalists

The Knight Center found that: "Journalists, especially those who work for local news outlets in cities that are most affected by drug violence have become the preferred targets of criminal organizations. Pressures, beatings, kidnappings, torture and killing are all tools that are frequently used to intimidate and silence independent investigations into drug trafficking in certain zones and its relationship with power" (Medel, 2010). Cartel censorship and control is enforced with threats, attacks, and bribes (CPJ, 2010, p. 16).

Not only do the cartels seek silence and impunity, they increasingly seek to influence perception, using a type of "narco-propaganda." This strategy employs a range of tools. These include both violent means—beheadings, *levantóns* (kidnappings), assassinations, bombings and grenade attacks—and informational means—*narcomantas* (banners), *narcobloqueos* (blockades), *manifestacións* (orchestrated demonstrations), and *narcocorridos* (or folk songs extolling cartel virtues). Simple methods such as graffiti and roadside signs are now amplified with digital media.

As a consequence, the cartels employ a virtual "public relations" or "information operations" branch to further their economic and increasingly tangible political goals. In some cases (for example La Familia Michoacana) cartels are trying to assume the mantle of "social bandit" (Hobsbawn, 1969) to secure public support to thwart government counter-cartel initiatives. President Felipe Calderón warned that this interference or manipulation has become a threat to democracy and press freedom as cartels seek to impose their will and challenge the state and civil society. According to Calderón, "Now the great threat to freedom of expression in our country, and in other parts of the world without a doubt is organized crime."

Journalists' Impressions

I conducted a small sample of telephonic and e-interviews of journalists to gain an appreciation of the situation's impact and context. Carlos Rosales, a producer at an El Paso television news outlet suggested that attacks on journalists were not necessarily chilling reportage, but were "impacting the reporting of cartel related incidents." He noted that in Juàrez (which has experienced 3,000 cartel killings so far this year) "many journalists no longer apply their byline to stories in newspapers about drug cartels." Rosales also observed that "Some Mexican newsblogs run their operations from El Paso." Finally, Rosales commented that "Truth is the first casualty of war and the drug war has taken its toll on reporting, from journalists' lives to lack of reporting on incidents that impact the way governments are run" (Rosales, 2010).

Terry Poppa, author of *Drug Lord*, believes that attacks on journalists, such as ambushes are instrumental. "While they are not new, they are getting worse." Their purpose is "to silence the media and reign as anonymous as possible." Poppa believes media reportage is slowed by interference from cartels and that attacks obscure understanding of the situation. Poppa suggests that "citizen media" is a response to the attacks on formal journalistic outlets (Poppa, 2010).

Ioan Grillo, a print, radio, and video journalist in Mexico City, noted that "Attacks on journalists are having a definite effect on reporting by Mexican journalists especially in the hardest hit areas." The attacks have made "journalists refrain from using bylines, refrain from naming sources, hold back from investigating," and in "some cases refuse to report stories altogether." Grillo observes that "Cartels are shaping reportage by bribing journalists, by producing videos that they post on the Internet or give media, by the use of *narcomantas*, and by the use of extraordinary acts of violence that is often designed for media impact." Finally, he notes that "new media" is a popular "alternative to mainstream media to communicate attacks, shootouts, etc." in hard hit areas (Grillo, 2010).

Additional ethnographic study along the lines of Campbell's *Drug War Zone, Frontline Dispatches from the Streets of El Paso and Juárez* is warranted.

A New Communication Space?

As Tracy Wilkinson (2010) reported in the *Los Angeles Times*, journalists are under siege, causing reporters to "practice a profound form of self-censorship, or censorship imposed by the narcos." As a result, many reports assert that social media, Twitter, YouTube, and blogs—such as *El Blog del Narco*—are taking the place of traditional media. Wilkinson notes that in Reynosa the city is virtually under siege, with cartels dictating media coverage. She adds, "Throughout the state of Tamaulipas, in fact, journalists practice a profound form of self-censorship, or censorship imposed by the narcos... It is also the only place [thus far] where reporters with international news media have been confronted by gunmen and ordered to leave." According to Wilkinson, "Social media networks such as Twitter have taken the place of newspapers and radio reports, with everyone from security officials to regular people tweeting alerts about a gun battle here, a blockade there."

As a consequence of the battle to control information, journalists, the public, and the cartels themselves have embraced "new media" technologies (*i.e.,* social networking sites, Twitter, blogs, and other forms of horizontal self-communication). According to *Latin America News Dispatch* (O'Reilly, 2010), "people have been using blogs and Twitter accounts to cover what many of Mexico's mainstream media outlets will not. *El Blog del Narco* is one of the most notable of these outlets, according to its administrator, it receives four million visitors a week" (O'Reilly, 2010).

El Blog del Narco (http://www.blogdelnarco.com) which was established in March 2010 (Tuckman, 2010) also maintains a Facebook page. As of 14 December 2010, the page has logged 25,853 persons that "liked" the site. The site's Twitter account "Infonarco" has registered 2,648 Tweets; 29,071 followers; and 755 "listed" on the same date. Other notable Twitter feeds covering the narco-conflict include "gabrielregino" with 53,080 Tweets; 6,876 followers; and 357 "listed" and "Narcomexico" with 2,143 Tweets; 2,678 followers; and 99 "listed" (on 14 December 2010).

According to the Knight Center (Medel, 2010, p. 23) a reaction to official news control or manipulation has stimulated cartel info ops: "A recent twist on this tight control has been the emergence of organized crime groups trying—successfully—to dictate the news agenda and impose restrictions that reaches the public." This narco-info includes intimidation and pressure: "These threats come in public statements, as well as via social networks, Internet chat rooms, e-mail, and their own news releases" (Medel, 2010, p. 23). As we have seen, some of this interference and pressure has led to complete or partial news blackouts in Mexico's contested regions. In areas subject to blackouts, social media and information communications technology (ICT) appears to be filling the vacuum. Again from the Knight Center, "Before the foreign press revealed what was happening in Tamaulipas, the media blackout was broken by residents of the affected towns. Armed with video cameras and cell phones, they filmed the drug smugglers roadside checkpoints, hundreds of bullet shells on the ground after shootouts, and shoes strewn in the streets, which raised the question of what happened to their owners" (Madel, 2010, p. 24).

In the current drug war, we see ICT and "new media" filling a variety of roles for a variety of actors. The traditional media uses social media to facilitate reportage and transmit information around blockades (for example from Cd. Juárez to El Paso); bloggers and Twitter reporters use it to transmit stories; and the cartels themselves use social media and ICT to project their information platforms. This situation amounts to one where a range of social actors are engaged in what Castells (2007, 2009) calls a "power-counter-power" conflict where communication and power relationships are shaping a new communication space within the network society. This new informational space includes efforts by cartels to cast themselves in the mantle of community protector or social bandit (Hobsbawm, 1969).

Conclusion

Mexico's cartels are increasingly using refined information operations (info ops) to wage their war against each other and the Mexican state. These info ops include the calculated use of instrumental and symbolic violence to shape the conflict environment. The result: attacks on media outlets, and kidnappings and assassinations of journalists by narco-cartels to obscure operations and silence critics. Editors and journalists turn to self-censorship to protect themselves; others have become virtual mouthpieces for the gangs and cartels, only publishing materials the cartels approve. Cartels are now beginning to issue press releases to control the information space—through censorship and cartel co-option of reportage. Finally, the public, government and even cartels are increasingly using new media (horizontal means of mass self-communication) to influence and understand the raging criminal insurgencies.

Special thanks to Fundación MEPI; Reporters Sans Frontiéres; and Trans-Border Institute, University of San Diego for allowing the reprint of their figures in this work

CHAPTER 15

EXTREME BARBARISM, A DEATH CULT, AND HOLY WARRIORS IN MEXICO: SOCIETAL WARFARE SOUTH OF THE BORDER?

Robert J. Bunker and John P. Sullivan
Initially published May 22, 2011

THIS SHORT ESSAY IS about impression—gut feelings combined with a certain amount of analytical skill—about recent trends taking place in Mexico concerning the ongoing criminal insurgencies being waged by the various warring cartels, gangs, and mercenary organizations that have metastasized though out that nation (and in many other regions as well). The authors spent over eight hours sequestered together about a month ago on a five-hundred mile 'there and back again road trip' to attend a training conference as instructors for the Kern County Chiefs of Police. Our talks centered on Mexican Drug Cartels, 3rd Generation Gangs, 3rd Phase Cartels, Criminal Insurgency Theory, and a host of related topics most folks just don't normally discuss in polite company. In the car, and at the conference, we were bombarded by Sullivan's never ending twitter and social networking news feeds—in Spanish and English—linked to the criminal violence in Mexico. If Dante had been our contemporary, we fear, he could just have easily taken a stroll through some of the cities and towns of Mexico using those news feeds and substituting the imagery for the circles of hell he described in his early 14th century work the *Divine Comedy*.

The hours of conversation about the conflicts in Mexico, bolstered by the news feeds and even the Q&A from the training time provided to the Kern Chiefs, provided us both with much to reflect upon. Additionally, both authors are currently co-writing three essays for a follow-on project to the earlier *Narcos Over the Border* (Routledge) book, the work that zenpundit.com found as "...one of the more disturbing academic works recently published in the national security field, not excluding even those monographs dealing with Islamist terrorism and Pakistan," concerning Mexico's immense problems.[1] If this were not enough, as part of our ongoing collaboration, the authors have been trying to determine what to make of Hazen's June 2010 *International Review of the Red Cross* paper "Understanding gangs as armed groups."[2] Her conclusions just don't correlate with the empirical evidence stemming from the cartel and gang related incidents regularly occurring in Mexico. That work suggests to us that American street gang researchers, whose work Hazen utilized as the basis of her analysis, are totally insulated from the reality of the conflicts in Mexico—just as are many members of the American public and their elected officials. For good or for bad, we are not so well insulated, having tracked what has been taking place in that country for some years now. The ongoing review (for the purposes of identifying cartel tattoos, cult icons, and instances of ritual killing) of the images of the tortured and broken bodies—some no longer recognizable as once ever being human beings— continually haunts us both.

Our impression is that what is now taking place in Mexico has for some time gone way beyond secular and criminal (economic) activities as defined by traditional organized crime studies.[3] In fact, the intensity of change may indeed be increasing. Not only have *de facto political* elements come to the fore—*i.e.,* when a cartel takes over an entire city or town, they have no choice but to take over political functions formerly administered by the local government— but social (*narcocultura*) and religious/spiritual (*narcocultos*) characteristics are now making themselves more pronounced. What we are likely witnessing is Mexican society starting to not only unravel but to go to war with itself. The bonds and relationships that hold that society together are fraying, unraveling, and, in some instances, the polarity is reversing itself with trust being replaced by mistrust and suspicion. Traditional Mexican values and competing criminal value systems are engaged in a brutal contest over the 'hearts, minds, and souls' of its citizens in a street-by-street, block-by-block, and city-by-city war over the future social and political organization of Mexico. Environmental modification is taking place in some urban centers and rural outposts as deviant norms replace traditional ones and the younger generation fully accepts a criminal value system as their baseline of behavior because they have known no other. The continuing incidents of ever increasing barbarism—some would call this a manifestation of evil even if secularly motivated—and the growing popularity of a death cult are but two examples of this clash of values. Additionally, the early rise of what appears to be cartel holy warriors may now also be taking place. While extreme barbarism, death cults, and possibly now holy warriors found in the Mexican cartel wars are still somewhat the exception rather than the rule, each of these trends is extremely alarming, and will be touched upon in turn.

Extreme Barbarism

The 8 March 2011 video highlighted under the article "Narco Execution Videos and its Effects on the Population in General" is about as bad as it gets:

> This video surfaced today on the narco blogs, its content is extremely violent. It is unknown exactly when it was filmed, nor where it took place.
>
> The film lasts seven minutes, in which a group of masked men in military style clothing have hung a man by his feet. This person was clearly still alive when the assailants castrated him. Music can be heard playing in the background as one of the men step in and strategically peels back the face and skin of the victim before decapitating him. After it is over, the people standing around joke and laugh while they take cell pictures of this gruesome act. The video ends with the body being hacked up into pieces, and put into black plastic trash bags.[4]

Torture-killings have been part and parcel of the drug wars in Mexico but the level of brutality now appears very much to be in a sustained pattern. Since that video has aired, a number of other heinous acts have been chronicled in these additionally selected *Borderland Beat* (http://www.borderlandbeat.com/) postings. Just a few examples from early April quickly portray the horrors taking place in Mexico on an increasingly common basis:

- 5 April 2011: Several narco blogs have recently released a video showing a young blond haired woman decapitating a man whose head and hands are bound with what appears to be duct tape. It is unknown where and when the 14-minute video was made. During the video you can hear unidentified men advise the woman on how to perform the beheading, as well as their concerns that the event be documented properly on video. As the woman continues severing the victim's head with a machete, you can hear an unidentified man refer to her as "La Guera Loca" (the crazy blond), while another man says "This is what happens to those who help the Zetas." After the woman finishes the decapitation and briefly poses with the head as a trophy, others begin to dismember the victim's body and skin the face and skull.

- 7 April 2011: Two men were recently found brutally murdered and posed in front of a shop in the Guadalupe neighborhood of Tepic, Nayarit. According to preliminary reports, the men were both skinned alive before their hearts were removed. At this time, neither man has been identified. *Note: This is somewhat reminiscent of an alleged Los Zetas incident that took place earlier— "…a June 6, 2010, torture/mass murder where six victims were found in a Cancun cave with their hearts cut out and "Z" carved in their abdomens…"*[5]

- 8 April 2011: Wednesday afternoon, 42 year old Roberto Abarca Serna, a Social Science professor at the University Autonomous of Guerrerro and the founder of Carrizo Theater Company, was kidnapped outside his home in Acapulco by a group of armed gunmen. The kidnappers called Abarco Serna's wife and demanded a $40,000 pesos [US dollar equivalent not specified] ransom for his release. When his wife, Citlalli Delgado Galdino, took the money to her husband's kidnappers, she too was taken by force. The kidnappers tied Ms Delgado to a chair and forced her to watch as they beheaded her husband.

- 11 April 2011: Army troops found 16 more bodies in the mass graves outside the northern city of San Fernando, raising the total number of bodies discovered to 88, the Mexican Defense Secretariat said. *Note: These mass graves, and others like them in Northern Mexico, are now yielding hundreds of bodies of innocent victims likely killed by Los Zetas enforcers, the majority of which were Central Americans riding buses up North as they attempted to migrate to the US.*

This list could go on and on with dozens of similar incidents chronicled over the last month—the majority of them only reported in the Mexican press and never translated into English—with many times that number never even reported because of the impunity provided to those who commit such heinous acts. It is said that less than 2% of those who engage in criminal acts in Mexico are ever convicted and sentenced for their crimes.[6] The incidents of maiming, torture, and brutality are simply not subsiding in Mexico and anyone who says otherwise is not actually monitoring the violence that is taking place on a daily basis. It is of little wonder that many towns in Northern Mexico have been depopulated, with businesses and residences burned down and others boarded up and abandoned by their owners. While this is getting little traction in the US press, Mexico is starting to see internally displaced populations related to narco and criminal violence now estimated to be in excess of 200,000 individuals.[7]

A Death Cult

Increasingly, stories and reports are being written on *Santa Muerte*—the Death Saint—indigenous to Mexico though also now found in the United States and in Central America. This unsanctioned quasi-Catholic saint has in the past been worshiped as a 'grim reaper' type figure by marginal elements—peasants, the urban poor, and criminals—in Mexican society. Offerings of flowers, fruits, corn, beer, and other commodities, along with petitions for good health, luck with love, and even coming into wealth have been made at *Santa Muerte* altars. Often, the images of Jesus, the Virgin, and the saints of last resort (such as Judas Tadeo) would be found together with images of the death saint. Rainbow colors and lighter candle shades (representative of more benign candle magic spells) had dominated in the past though a harsher gray area element had always existed that focused on cursing others, defending against spells, and protecting oneself from being arrested or being sentenced to prison. Many times the images of other unsanctioned saints, such as *Jesus Malverde* and *Juan Soldado*, are also found in tandem with that of *Santa Muerte* in the possession of the harsher gray area worshipers who engage in criminal activities.

While this saint has been around for over five decades, a narco-criminal variant has since emerged that has elevated *Santa Muerte* into a dark and vengeful deity in her own right. This variant of *Santa Muerte* has nothing even remotely to do with Catholicism and is rapidly gaining adherents. The total number of *Santa Muerte* worshipers is somewhere in the low millions with the actual breakdown along the continuum of belief— traditional, gray area, and the darker narco-criminal variant— unknown. An educated guess would be that the traditional and gray area believers still dominate but as *narcocultura* spreads, especially amongst the young in Mexico, more worshipers will continue to gravitate to the harsher aspects of the faith.

What is known is that the darker variant of *Santa Muerte* is by no means benign and that simple commodities are unacceptable as offerings. Dark altars laden with weapons, money, narcotics, and sometimes stained with blood have been identified. The stakes have been raised now that petitions to cause agonizing death to one's enemies and bless cartel operatives before battle are being made, in essence providing them spiritual armor against other criminal forces and Mexican authorities. Human body parts and bowls of blood left at *Santa Muerte* altars, both public and private, are becoming more common as are actual human sacrifices and the ritualized dismemberment of the dead. Examples of what appear to be death cult sacrifices, rituals, and activities include:

- The stacking of headless bodies and the staged placement of body parts. One grisly incident photo shows a skinned skull resting on severed arms with the victim's male genitalia held in the palm of one of their hands.
- Decapitated heads left at the tombs of deceased drug lords— implicated as *Santa Muerte* worshipers— as sacrificial offerings.
- Decapitated heads offered directly to *Santa Muerte* by her worshipers.
- Victims killed at *Santa Muerte* altars/shrines.

- The ritual burning of decapitated heads as offerings.
- The removal of the hearts of victims.
- The skinning of victims while alive.
- The likely desecration of shrines belonging to more benign Saints.
- The use of black candle magic to request that the deity kill one's enemies.
- The threatening of a kidnap victim at a *Santa Muerte* altar with divine wrath if they failed to cooperate with their captors.
- The alleged smoking of a victim's ashes mixed with cocaine in a 'smoking death' ritual.[8]

The authors are well aware of the old 'Satanic panic' scare of much of the 1980s and how, for a time, Satanists and their covens were thought to be lurking near practically every preschool in the US so our intent is not to overplay the threat posed by the narco-criminal variant of *Santa Muerte*.[9] On the other hand, organized cartel groups, such as *Los Zetas*, and members of independent kidnap/kill teams, such as the one that engaged in the Chandler, Arizona beheading in late 2010, have increasingly become followers of this dark and vengeful deity. Tattoos of *Santa Muerte* have been found on their operatives, altars and other icons have been found in their possession, and their members have been tied to death cult sacrifices and rituals. Even *Santa Muerte* high priest David Romo has been linked to a *Los Zetas* kidnapping cell and related criminal activities.[10] Additionally, quite a few incidents are known only to Mexican and US law enforcement and have not been widely reported in the press or have been filed as news stories that have been quickly forgotten. Example of the latter are the April 2011 *Santa Muerte* worshipers linked to killings in Chicago—some of the victims had their throats cut while bound— and the January 2010 human sacrifice that took place in Ciudad Juarez.[11]

To suggest that at least a thousand heavily armed and increasingly fanatical *Santa Muerte* followers of the narco-criminal variant, with blood on their hands, and at times on their altars, now exist simply cannot be disputed. That would mean that only 1-in-13 to 1-in-15 of the estimated 13,000 to 15,000 *Los Zetas* hard-core operatives—less than 10% of them—have become death cult followers; a ridiculously low estimate given what we know of *Los Zetas* training and indoctrination profiles.[12]

Holy Warriors

La Familia Michoacana (LFM), one of the dominant cartels in Mexico with thousands of members, is an evangelical-criminal organization based on a bizarre fusion of Christian teachings, the writings of John Eldredge (*Wild at Heart* et al.), and the teachings of the original La Familia leadership. Catechisms and doctrine have been produced by "El Más Loco" (The Craziest One) and others. They help to facilitate the indoctrination of new recruits and guide them through the stages of spiritual passage as they advance within the ranks of the cartel. Symbolism and icons utilized by cartel members include crucifixes, rosaries, the LFM tattoo, and related *narcocultra* adornments. Many of the brothers and sisters who belong to the cartel are considered 'saved souls' salvaged from the streets and from drug and alcohol rehabilitation centers and, once indoctrinated as true believers, can be considered adherents of a militarized form of pseudo-Christianity. Past allegations of cartel ties to the New Jerusalem Movement in Mexico and related apocalyptic beliefs have been made concerning LFM.[13]

La Familia has thus always been a cult based organization and steeped in notions of 'Divine Justice.' In September 2006, LFM threw five severed heads onto the *Sol y Sombra* nightclub floor with the accompanying narcobanner (*narcomanta*) "The family doesn't kill for money. It doesn't kill for women. It doesn't kill innocent people, only those who deserve to die. Know that this is divine justice."[14] In January 2010, the group was accused of sewing a victim's face onto a soccer ball though it just as likely could have been the work of an allied cartel with a pronounced sense of sick humor.[15] Still, the ritualized violence which forms the basis of control through fear exercised by this cartel even runs though basic aspects of its enforcer training:

In mid-2010 Miguel "El Tyson" Ortiz Miranda, a captured La Familia activist, described the training of the organization's potential hitmen. He said that a group of 40 are taken to Jesús del Monte, a mountainous zone, and are directed to pursue, shoot, and cook 15 victims. This exercise tests whether recruits can conquer their fear and overcome the sight of their quarries' blood.[16]

Additionally, dismembered bodies with LFM carved into them and dumped onto the streets is a not-uncommon occurrence in Michoacana and other cartel controlled territories. The beating of sinners with barbed wire wrapped boards and whips—their backs flayed and bloodied—has also been reported. In fact, LFM has imposed its own criminal-spiritual based law in its territories— essentially a pseudo-Christian equivalent to Sharia Law found in Islamist lands that has meted out harsh punishments to teenagers wearing sagging pants, hairnets, and who have engaged in other undesirable activities. Furthermore, Catholic priests who challenge LFM dictates have been subjected to death threats.

La Familia Michoacana has been taking a pounding of late with much of its senior leadership now killed or captured. The targeting of this cartel has become a Mexican Government priority since it is considered every bit as dangerous as *Los Zetas* cartel. Many media commentators, and even some researchers, have suggested that the cartel is on the verge of disintegration. Indeed, LFM called for a truce with the Mexican Government and finally disbanded were in January 2011 by means of their own pronouncement via numerous *narcomantas*. Still, at the legacy middle management and lower levels, the former LFM cadre remain relatively unscathed and still exert much control over Michocana and the other former territories.

This crisis of leadership in LFM, however, has recently resulted in a new cartel appearing in Michoacana. The new cartel— *Los Caballeros Templarios* (Knights Templars)— appeared in March 2011 and proclaimed itself the successor to LFM by means of over thirty *narcomantas*.[17] In truth, it is unknown if the entire cadre of the cartel itself has morphed into *Los Caballeros Templarios* or if only a large splinter faction of *La Familia* has decided to establish this new organization. What is clear is the name and iconitry behind this new cartel directly invokes Christian Medieval symbolism pertaining to God's holy warriors. This is highly significant and elevates the central cartel tenet of 'Divine Justice' to an even more pronounced level than that initially promoted by LFM. The Knights Templars (aka Knighthood of the Temple of Solomon) a military-religious order, were the Papacy's mid-12th to late-13th century shock troops in the Holy Land and were known not only for their piety but for their bloodlust in battle against the infidel.

Los Caballeros Templarios, so the rhetoric goes, would thus represent a 21st century criminal-military-religious order that views itself as the protectors of the people of Michoacana. While many consider such rhetoric nothing more than a sham, enough true believers have already been indoctrinated to require that we take the rise of such a cult-like order as a very serious development. The English translation of the narcobanners proclaiming the rise of this cartel is as follows:

> To the society of Michoacan we inform you that from today we will be working here on the altruistic activities that were previously performed by the Familia Michoacana, we will be at the service of Michoacan society to attend to any situation which threatens the safety of the Michoacanos.

> Our commitment to society will be: to safeguard order; avoid robberies, kidnappings, extortion; and to shield the state from possible rival intrusions.

> *Sincerely, The Knights Templar*[18]

Numerous text only based *narcomantas* tied to and set next to victims murdered by this cartel—hanging from bridges and trees, placed in chairs, and dumped on the street— have already turned up over the last few months. Iconitry is also already appearing for this new cartel that includes the *Templarios* name with a shield with a red cross, a white battle flag with a white cross, and an armored knight holding a sword. To date, no *Templarios* tattoos specifically relating to cartel members have been identified on corpses or on former LFM members that have been captured in news or in blog photos, however, that too will come if this new cartel survives into the future.

Conclusions

Whether we are now catching glimpses of societal warfare actually breaking out south of the US-Mexican border, *i.e.*, between traditional Mexican society and that of criminal insurgents, we will leave the reader to consider. What we wish to do here is identify three major concerns, derived from very dark forms of spirituality, that pertain to the incidents of extreme barbarism, the rise of a death cult, and the emergence of holy warriors in Mexico that are deeply troubling to us:

- The continuing forms of extreme barbarism evident in the torture and killings of cartel and gang victims in Mexico is creating a growing cadre of hardened killers; some of whom are still in their childhoods. While most of these killings are secular in nature, the very participation in such acts of barbarism will forever change a person. This goes beyond 'the dark stain left on the soul' religious arguments which may have their own merits to focus on the fact that a growing number of cartel and gang enforcers in Mexico are actively engaging in, and becoming accustomed to, sociopathic behaviors reminiscent of serial killers. Skinning people, cutting out their hearts, castrating them or cutting off their breasts, throwing them in a vat of acid, or setting them on fire *while they are alive* is incrementally becoming more accepted in *narcocultura* as a means of settling scores and doing away with ones' enemies. What this will eventually mean for Mexican society is unknown but the value system of these hardened killers, and what spirituality they may eventually gravitate to, will directly be in conflict with anything resembling Mexican civil society.

- There are documented incidents of ritual killing, human sacrifice, and petitions for divine intervention (such as death magic) in Mexico tied to the narco-criminal version of *Santa Muerte*. The removal of hearts, the offering of a human heads, the leaving of the dead as offerings at public shrines, the ritual burning of heads, and altars found with bowls of blood in them suggest *Santa Muerte* has indeed become an increasingly powerful deity in her own right to those that worship her. The call for Holy War by *Santa Muerte* high priest David Romo, linked to Los Zetas, as a result of the wholesale destruction of Santa Muerte temples by the Mexican government in Northern Mexico is also alarming as is *Los Zetas* cartel's increasing embrace of the death saint as their spiritual patron and divine benefactor. What the future holds for this death cult is unknown, but it is not good for Mexico, and the massive growth of its narco-criminal variant suggests many new worshippers are now praying at her dark altars.

- A self-sacrifice component of the holy warrior archetype may be emerging as the ideology of the new *Los Caballeros*

Templarios cartel evolves. While we never thought we would consider this as a potential in Mexico, the possibility of future *Templarios* suicide (martyrdom) operations—likely based on active-aggressor assaults to kill high value targets such as Mexican governmental officials responsible for targeting this cartel— has to now be at least contemplated. Human sacrifice to God in this instance, unlike that of the emerging death cult in Mexico, is derived from ones' own spilling of blood as a martyr and not the spilling of your victim's blood. Since car bomb use in Mexico has been relatively restrained to date, no expectation currently exists that *Templarios* martyrdom operations will employ VBIEDs in the near term, but such operations could conceivably at some point come to pass.

The Thirty Years' War in Europe (1618-1648) was known for its sheer brutality and in many ways represented a conflict between the old Medieval order and something entirely new. Heinous and barbaric acts and mass depopulation ensued due to a conflict that took on religious overtones. We now wonder what historians will someday say about the Narco-Criminal Wars in Mexico (2006-?) and those social and political forms that emerge from the ashes of a broadening conflict now taking place south of our border. While that which is taking place in Mexico is nowhere near the horrors of the Thirty Years' War, a death toll of 40,000 is fast approaching and new forms of dark spirituality are now being injected into what heretofore has been considered only criminal, hence secular, insurgencies taking place. Mexico's new '*narcocultura*' as embodied in *narcocorridos* (songs glorifying narcotraffickers) and the saints of the new cults or 'narco-religions' have profound potentials for the soul and social fabric of a nation.[19]

AFTERWORD:
MEXICO: A MOSAIC CARTEL WAR

Paul Rexton Kan
Initially published June 12, 2011

A SITUATION OF HIGH-INTENSITY crime does not mean that a war is not occurring in Mexico. But it is a war of a different kind. In fact, there are several conflicts occurring at once that blend into each other. There is the conflict of cartels among each other, the conflict within cartels, cartels against the Mexican state, cartels and gangs against the Mexican people and gangs versus gangs. When combined, they form a mosaic cartel war that creates an atmosphere "somewhere between Al Capone's Chicago and an outright war".[1] It is not an irregular or regular war; neither is it a small war nor a general war, nor a limited war, nor a total war, nor any of the familiar appellations given to armed conflicts fought by conventional militaries. And, finally it is not "a war about nothing."[2] It is a multidimensional, multiparty and multi-location armed conflict fought among criminal groups over what are essentially criminal goals; the groups are resisted by the state while their goals are rejected by it, making the state a party to the conflict.

Because it is a war of a different kind, the targets of the cartels have been wide ranging— from police to journalists, from clinics to discos, military bases to children's birthday parties. "Criminal cleansing" has occurred in Mexican towns where cartels have ordered residents to leave or face possible death. A mosaic cartel war is complex in its manifestation and confounding to traditional military and law enforcement solutions.

As a result, there is great difficulty for governments on either side of the border to fight this type of war and to bring the violence under control. As RT Naylor argues, "the violence of the state is often a response to the violence of the criminal; the reverse is also true. And once the interactive cycle of violence is set in motion, it may be impossible to separate action from reaction, or to say for sure if the reduction in the use of violence on one side will lead to the same on the other."[3] This frustration over cause and effect is part of the reason that many have used inappropriate labels from other types of conflicts to describe the situation in Mexico. An alternative conception is required to more accurately describe and assess the current outbreak of a mosaic cartel war in Mexico, its dynamics and its potential end.

The Violence of High-Intensity Crime: War of All against All

The lumping together of insurgents, terrorists and organized criminal syndicates under the overly broad category of non-state actors adds little analytical clarity. Defining a term in opposition to another term—such as non-state as opposed to state—is conceptually murky. Many disparate groups can be classified as non-state actors, ranging from multinational corporations to civic organizations. Adding the qualifier of "violent" does little to ease the confusion because violent non-state actors can include sea going pirates as well as private military companies. The term "network" is more descriptive than non-state actor. It refers to the structure and operation of a group, but once again it encompasses a wide variety of groups that are both legal and illegal. The term "dark network" focuses on how non-hierarchical, dispersed social structures are used for criminal ends.[4] While a useful improvement, it fails to capture many of the dynamics and pressures that the actors face in dark networks and why they choose to use violence.

To sharpen the focus, it is important to understand why differing groups are organized and under what conditions they use collective violence in order to achieve a particular goal or set of goals. In Mexico, high-intensity crime is occurring due to a war waged by violent entrepreneurs who seek to prevail over one another and the state in a hypercompetitive illegal market in order to control it or a particular portion of it. Violent entrepreneurs are mostly private groups that create "a set of organizational solutions and action strategies enabling organized force (or organized violence) to be converted into money or other valuable assets on a permanent basis....Violent entrepreneurship is a means of increasing the private income of the wielders of force through ongoing relations of exchange with other groups that own other resources."[5] Cartels are a type of violent entrepreneur because they derive their income from the use of force to prevail in private activities that are highly circumscribed or prohibited by the state. For violent entrepreneurs, the use of force is the extension of private profit making, rather than the extension of a political agenda. Violence itself is a means, not an end; it is "a resource, not the final product."[6] As a resource, violence is used by cartels to insure that the product, which is illegal in nature, is delivered to its client base so that profits can be derived.

NOTES

PREFACE:
A SINALOAN KINGPIN, A REPORTER, AND THE
REALITY OF MEXICAN STATE SOVEREIGNTY

1. This essay is a short excerpt from Max Manwaring, *A 'New' Dynamic in the Western Hemisphere Security Environment: The Mexican Zetas and Other Private Armies*. Carlisle, PA: US Army War College, September 2009, 26-32. The views expressed here do not represent those of the U.S. Army, Department of Defense or the U.S. Government.
2. Nathan Vardi, "Joaquin Guzman Has Become The Biggest Drug Lord Ever." *Forbes* (15 July 2011), http://blogs.forbes.com/nathanvardi/2011/06/15/joaquin-guzman-has-become-the-biggest-drug-lord-ever/.
3. The following vignette is taken from Guy Lawson, 'The War Next Door', *Rolling Stone*, 13 November 2008.
4. Mark Stevenson, 'Top Mexico Cops Charged with Favoring Drug Cartel', Associated Press (24 January 2009), www.news.yahoo.com.

CHAPTER 1: IRAQ & THE AMERICAS:
3 GEN GANGS LESSONS AND PROSPECTS

1. For an overview and literature survey of this topic see John P. Sullivan and Robert J. Bunker, "Third Generation Gang

Studies: An Introduction", *Journal of Gang Research*, Vol. 14. No. 4. Summer 2007, pp. 1-10.

2. A perspective on the Red Brigades as a 3 GEN Gang can be found in Max G. Manwaring, "Gangs and Coups D' Streets in the New World Disorder: Protean Insurgents in Post-Modern War", Robert J. Bunker, ed., Criminal-States and Criminal-Soldiers, special double issue of *Global Crime*, Vol. 7. No. 3-4. August/November 2006; for drug cartel and warlord similarities to 3 GEN Gangs see John P. Sullivan and Robert J. Bunker, "Drug Cartels, Street Gangs, and Warlords", Robert J. Bunker, ed., Non-State Threats and Future Wars, special issue of *Small Wars & Insurgencies*, Vol. 13. No. 2. Summer 2002, pp. 40-53.

3. Actual numbers of Iraqis killed each month and total figures are unknown. Sources are unreliable and typically inflated or deflated in order to benefit the policies or agenda of the group providing the statistics. We can safely say that 1,000 to 2,000 people are being killed each month but the upper limit of 5,000 people is no longer out of the range of possibility given the high levels of violence now generated by the simultaneous insurgency and civil war taking place. Iraqi casualty reports and tracking websites offer total numbers killed upwards from 50,000.

4. Malcolm W. Klein, *The American Street Gang*, Oxford: Oxford University Press, 1995, pp. 92-95.

5. Los Angeles County gang homicide information provided by Sgt. Wes McBride, Los Angeles Sheriff's Department, Retired, Safe Streets Bureau.

6. Statement of Chris Swecker, Assistant Director, Criminal Investigative Division Federal Bureau of Investigation Before the Subcommittee on the Western Hemisphere House International Relations Committee April 20, 2005.

7. See Ana Arana, "How the Street Gangs Took Central America," *Foreign Affairs*, Vol. 84, No. 3. May/June 2005, pp. 98-110.

8. See Andrew Downie, "Police Are Targeted in Deadly Attacks, Prison Riots in Brazil", *Los Angeles Times*, Sunday, May 14, 2006, p. A25; Marcelo Soares and Patrick J. McDonnell, "Inmates Unleash a Torrent of Violence on Brazilian City", *Los Angeles Times*, Tuesday, May 16, 2006, pp. A1, A16;

and Marcelo Soares and Patrick J. McDonnell, "Death Toll in Sao Paulo Rise to 133; City is Calm", *Los Angeles Times*, Wednesday, May 17, 2006, p. A16.

9. See Lisa J. Campbell, "The Use of Beheadings by Fundamentalist Islam", Robert J. Bunker, ed., *Criminal-States and Criminal-Soldiers*, special double issue of Global Crime, Vol. 7. No. 3-4. August/November 2006.

10. The US military seems to think that temporarily raising troop levels in order to neutralize Muqtada al-Sadr's 'Mahdi Army' (Shia militia) and possibly launching an offensive into the Sunni stronghold of Al Anbar province in support of the Iraqi government offer the best hopes for victory. This plan is being debated within the government and already criticized in some quarters. See Julian E. Barnes, "Larger U.S. effort in Iraq is proposed", *Los Angeles Times*, Wednesday, December 13, 2006, pp. A1, A16; and Maura Reynolds, "Majority support pullout timeline", *Los Angeles Times*, Wednesday, December 13, 2006, pp. A17.

CHAPTER 2: STATE OF SIEGE: MEXICO'S CRIMINAL INSURGENCY

1. "Factbox— Mexican President Calderon's War on Drug Gangs," *Reuters*, March 16, 2008, http://uk.reuters.com/article/latestCrisis/idUKN1644494820080616 (Accessed 17 June 2008).

2. "Mexican Cartels 'Threaten State," *BBC*, July 14, 2008, http://news.bbc.co.uk/2/hi/americas/7506581.stm (Accessed 5 August 2008).

3. See Enrique Krauze, Mexico, Biography of Power: A History of Modern Mexico 18101996 (New York: Harper Perennial, 1998).

4. *Attacks on the Press in 2007*, Committee to Protect Journalists (New York: CPJ, 2008).

5. Jeremy Schwartz, "Judges Latest Target in Mexico Drug War," *Cox News Service*, February 2, 2008.

6. Graham Hall Turbeville Jr., "Outlaw Private Security Firms: Criminal and Terrorist Agendas Outnumber Private Security

Alternatives," in *Criminal-States and Criminal Soldiers*, (ed) Robert J. Bunker, (New York: Routledge, 2008, p. 243).

7. "CIA World Factbook—Mexico," Central Intelligence Agency, 10 June 2008, https://www.cia.gov/library/publications/the-world-factbook/geos/mx.html (Accessed 15 June 2008).

8. Ibid.

9. George Friedman, "Mexico: On the Road to a Failed State?" *Stratfor*, May 13, 2008.

10. Ibid.

11. For an example of "black globalization" in action see John Robb, "The Pull of Black Globalization in Afghanistan," *Global Guerrillas*, 20 December 2005, http://globalguerrillas. typepad.com/globalguerrillas/2005/12/journal_the_pul.html (Accessed 17 June 2008).

12. Moises Naim, *Illicit: How Smugglers, Traffickers, and Copycats Are Hijacking the Global Economy* (New York: Doubleday, 2005), quoted in John Robb, "Nation-States, Market-States, and Virtual-States," Robert J. Bunker (ed), *Criminal-States and Criminal Soldiers* (New York: Routledge, 2008, p. 31).

13. Ibid.

14. John P. Sullivan and Robert J. Bunker, "Drug Cartels, Street Gangs, and Warlords" in Robert J. Bunker (ed) *Non State Threats and Future Wars* (London: Frank Cass, 2003, p. 44).

15. Colleen W Cook, *Congressional Research Service Report for Congress: Mexico's Drug Cartels* (Washington: Library of Congress, October 16, 2007, p. 2).

16. Cook, p. 4.

17. Manuel Roig-Franzia, "U.S. Guns Behind Cartel Killings in Mexico," *Washington Post*, October 29, 2007, p. A01.

18. Third Generation street gangs (3 GEN gangs) operate across a wide spatial range, have a high level of sophistication, and have developed political aims (including the co-option or weakening of structures of governance. See John P. Sullivan, "Maras Morphing: Revisiting Third Generation Gangs," *Global Crime*, Vol. 7, No. 3-4, August-November 2006, pp. 487-504 and John P. Sullivan, "Transnational gangs: The Impact of Third Generation Gangs in Central America,'" *Air & Space Power Journal—Spanish Edition*, Second Trimester 2008.

19. See Adam Elkus, "Gangs, Terrorists, and Trade," *Foreign Policy in Focus*, April 12, 2007, http://www.fpif.org/fpiftxt/4144.
20. Cook, p. 9.
21. Roig-Franzia, "U.S. Guns Behind Cartel Killings in Mexico."
22. Ibid.
23. Sullivan and Bunker, p. 46.
24. See Laurie Freeman, *State of Siege: Drug-Related Violence and Corruption in Mexico* (Washington, DC: Washington Office on Latin America, 2006).
25. Cook, pp. 10-13.
26. "Factbox— Mexican President Calderon's War on Drug Gangs," *Reuters*, 16 June 2008, http://uk.reuters.com/article/latestCrisis/idUKN1644494820080616 (Accessed 17 June 2008).
27. James McKinley Jr., "Mexico Hits Drug Gangs With Full Fury of War," *New York Times*, January 22, 2008, http://www.nytimes.com/2008/01/22/world/Americas/22mexico.html?sq=Mexico&st=n yt&scp=30&pagewanted=print (Accessed 17 June 2008).
28. Kate Doyle, "Documents Reveal Pentagon's Scrutiny of Zapatistas and Mexican Military: Rebellion in Chiapas and Counterinsurgency," Interhemispheric Resource Center, April 19, 2004, http://americas.irc-online.org/am/1717 (Accessed 17 June 2008).
29. Military Injustice: Mexico's Failure to Punish Army Abuses (New York: Human Rights Watch, December 2001), http://www.hrw.org/reports/2001/mexico/ (Accessed 18 August 2008).
30. Roig-Franzia, "U.S. Guns Behind Cartel Killings in Mexico."
31. Laurence Iliff, "Cartel Blamed in Botched Mexico City Bombing," *Dallas Morning News*, February 28, 2008, http://www.dallasnews.com/sharedcontent/dws/news/world/mexico/stories/DNbombing_28int.ART.State.Edition1.45e8d7c.html (Accessed 17 June 2008.)
32. John Robb, "The Coming Urban Terror," *City Journal*, Summer 2007, Vol. 14, No. 3, http://city-journal.org/html/17_3_urban_terrorism.html (Accessed 18 June 2008).

33. William Landwiesche, "City of Fear," *Vanity Fair*, April 2007, http://www.vanityfair.com/politics/features/2007/04/langewiesche200704 (Accessed 18 June 2008).

34. James McKinley Jr., "Mexico's War on Drugs Kills Its Police," *New York Times*, May 28, 2008, http://www.nytimes.com/2008/05/26/world/americas/26mexico.html?ref=world&pagew anted=print (Accessed 17 June 2008).

35. McKinley Jr., "Mexico Hits Drug Gangs With Full Fury of War."

36. –"Mexico Says Drug Cartel Had Spy in the President's Office," *New York Times*, February 7, 2005, <http://www.nytimes.com/2005/02/07/international/americas/07aide.html?scp=5&sq=Me xico+Cartel&st=nyt (Accessed 22 June 2008).

37. "Drug Lords Go After Mexican Police," *New York Daily News*, May 19, 2008, http://www.nydailynews.com/news/us_world/2008/05/19/2008-0519_drug_lords _go_after_mexican_police_.html?print=1&page=all (Accessed 18 June 18 2008).

38. James McKinley Jr, "With Beheadings and Attacks, Drug Gangs Terrorize Mexico," *The New York Times*, October 26, 2006, http://www.nytimes.com/2006/10/26/ world/americas/26mexico.html?_r=1&oref=slogin (Accessed 22 June 2008).

39. "Mexico Town's Entire Police Force Quits in Fear of Assassination,*" Fox News*, May 23, 2008, http://www.foxnews.com/story/0,2933,357761,00.html (Accessed 22 June 2008).

40. Friedman, "Mexico: On the Road to a Failed State?"

41. Fred Burton and Scott Stewart, "The Fallout from Phoenix," *Stratfor*, July 2, 2008.

42. Lizbeth Diaz, "Mexican Drug Gang Turns to Kidnapping in U.S," *Reuters*, August 12, 2008, http://www.reuters.com/article/domesticNews/ idUSN1250256620080812?feedType=R SS&feedName=domesticNews (Accessed 18 August 2008).

43. Deborah Bonello, "The Merida Initiative Discussed," *Los Angeles Times*, August 5, 2008, http://latimesblogs.latimes.

com/laplaza/2008/07/draft-merida.html (Accessed 5 August 2008).

44. See Mark Bowden, *Killing Pablo: The Hunt for the World's Greatest Outlaw* (Washington: Atlantic Monthly Press, 2001).

45. John P. Sullivan and Keith Weston, "Afterward: Law Enforcement Response Strategies for Criminal-states and Criminal-soldiers, *Global Crime*, Vol. 7, No. 3-4 (August-November 2006), pp. 615-628.

46. The "border states" are comprised of the states of Arizona, Baja California, Chihuahua, Coahuila, Nuevo Leon, New Mexico, Sonora, Tamaulipas, and Texas.

47. Ralph Blumenthal, "What the Mexicans Might Learn from the Italians," *New York Times*, June 1, 2008, http://www.nytimes.com/2008/06/01/weekinreview/ 01blumenthal.html?_r=1&ref=week inreview&oref=slogin (Accessed 5 August 2008).

CHAPTER 3: PLAZAS FOR PROFIT: MEXICO'S CRIMINAL INSURGENCY

1. John P. Sullivan and Adam Elkus, "Mexico's Criminal Insurgency," *Small Wars Journal*, August 19, 2008, http://smallwarsjournal.com/blog/2008/08/state-of-siege-mexicos-crim.

2. For a sampling of this literature, see John P. Sullivan and Robert J. Bunker, "Drugs, Street Cartels, and Warlords," in Robert Bunker (ed), *Non-State Threats and Future Wars*, London: Frank Cass & Co, 2003. Steve Metz, *Rethinking Insurgency*, Carlisle Barracks: Strategic Studies Institute, 2007, Mark T. Clark, "Does Clausewitz Apply to Criminal-States and Gangs" in Robert J. Bunker (Ed.), *Criminal States and Criminal Soldiers*, New York: Routledge, 2008, Paul Collier, *The Bottom Billion: Why The Poorest Countries Are Failing And What Can Be Done About It*, Oxford: Oxford University Press, 2007.

3. Stephen Meiners, "Central America: An Emerging Role in the Drug Trade," *STRATFOR*, March 26, 2009, http://

www.stratfor.com/index.php?q=weekly/20090326_ central_america_emerging_role_drug_.

4. David Luhnow and Joel Millman, "Mexican Leader Prepares for Bloodier Drug Wars," *Wall Street Journal*, February 28, 2009, http://online.wsj.com/article/SB123578172247398103.html.

5. Marina Montemayor, "Retired general takes over Ciudad Juarez security," Associated Press, March 16, 2009.

6. Ken Ellingwood, "Abuse allegations rise against Mexican army," *Los Angeles Times*, March 21, 2009. http://www.latimes.com/news/nationworld/world/la-fg-mexico-army21-2009mar21,0,7218318.story.

7. George W. Grayson, "Los Zetas and other Mexican Cartels Target Military Personnel," *E-Notes*, Foreign Policy Research Institute, March 2009. http://www.fpri.org/enotes/200903.grayson.loszetasmilitary.html

8. Marc Lacey, "Mexico Fights Drug War and Itself," *New York Times*, March 29, 2009, http://www.nytimes.com/2009/03/30/world/americas/30mexico.html?pagewanted=1&_r=2&ref=world.

9. Tracy Wilkinson, "Mexico drug cartels buying public support," *Los Angeles Times*, March 13, 2009, http://www.latimes.com/news/nationworld/world/la-fg-monterrey-drugs-recruits1-2009mar13,0,7828779.story.

10. Olga R. Rodriguez, "AP IMPACT: With the Mexican army in the war on drugs, a temporary fix to a long-term problem," Associated Press, March 29, 2009.

11. "Study: More Than Half of Mexico's Municipal Cops Unfit for the Job," *Latin American Herald Tribune* (Caracas), March 14, 2009.

12. "US to boost Mexico border defence," *BBC*, 24 March 2009, http://news.bbc.co.uk/2/hi/americas/7961670.stm.

13. Grayson.

14. Peter Grant, "Mexico's drug barons and police locked in an increasingly violent battle for supremacy," *The Telegraph*, March 18, 2009, http://www.telegraph.co.uk /news/worldnews/centralamericaandthecaribbean/mexico/5010852/Mexicos-drugbarons-and-police-locked-in-an-increasingly-violent-battle-for-supremacy.html.

15. Traci Carl, "Progress in Mexico drug war is drenched in blood," Associated Press, March 10, 2009.
16. "Women, Two Men Murdered in Northern Mexico," *Latin American Herald Tribune* (Caracas), April 9, 2009, htp://www.laht.com/article.asp?Articleid =331505&categoryId=1t 409.
17. Ibid.
18. Sara A. Carter, "100,000 foot soldiers in Mexican cartels," *Washington Times*, March 3, 2009.
19. Samuel Logan, "Los Zetas: Evolution of a Criminal Organization," *International Relations and Security Network* (ETH Zurich), March 11, 2009.
20. Ken Ellingwood and Tracy Wilkinson, "Drug cartels' new weaponry means war," *Los Angeles Times*, March 13, 2009.
21. Ibid.
22. Ibid.
23. Hakim Hazim, "Santisma Muerte: A Troubling Trend in Radicalization," *GroupIntel Blog*, February 23, 2009, http://www.groupintel.com/2009/02/23/santisma-muerte-a-troubling-trend-in-radicalization/.
24. Jason Buch, "S.A. Native in Squad of Young Hit Men Sentenced to Life in Prison," *San Antonio News*, March 5, 2009, http://www.mysanantonio.com/news/SA_man_among_hit_men_sentenced_to_life.html.
25. Tony Kail, *Corrections.com*, "Santisima Muerte: Patron saint of security threat groups," August 9, 2007, http://www.corrections.com/news/article?articleid= 16090.
26. Bruce Daniels, "Who Is 'Santa Muerte'?," *Albuquerque News-Journal*, March 27, 2009, http://www.abqjournal.com/abqnews/abqnewseeker-mainmenu-39/11599-940am-who-is-santa-muerte.html.
27. John Burnett, "Mexican Drug Cartels Recruiting Young Men, Boys," *NPR*, March 24, 2009.
28. See P.W. Singer, *Children at War*, Los Angeles: University of California Press, 2006 and John P. Sullivan, "Child Soldiers: Despair, Barbarization, and Conflict," *Air & Space Power Journal* (Spanish Edition), March 2008, for a detailed discussion on children in organized armed violence.

29. Ivan Briscoe, "The Proliferation of the 'Parallel State,'" Madrid: Fundación para las Relaciones Internacionales y el Diálogo Exterior, October 13, 2008, p 2.

30. Fred Burton and Scott Stewart, "The Fallout from Phoenix," *STRATFOR*, July 2, 2008.

31. See John P. Sullivan and Adam Elkus, "Postcard from Mumbai: Modern Urban Siege," *Small Wars Journal*, February 16, 2009, http://smallwarsjournal.com/mag/ 2009/02/postcard-from-mumbai.php.

32. Ibid.

33. David Ronfeldt, "Why Mexico May NOT Fall Apart," *Apropos of Two Theories*, March 30, 2009, http://twotheories.blogspot.com/2009/03/why-mexico-may-not-fall-apart-and-way.

CHAPTER 4: FUTURE CONFLICT: CRIMINAL INSURGENCIES, GANGS AND INTELLIGENCE

1. This paper was originally presented to the Panel on Patterns of Conflict: Future Threat Analysis Intelligence Studies Section, International Studies Association, 50th ISA Annual Convention. New York, NY, 18 February 2009.

2. Martin van Creveld, *The Transformation of War*, New York: The Free Press, 1991.

3. John P. Sullivan and Adam Elkus, "Red Teaming Criminal Insurgency," *Red Team Journal*, 30 January 2009 at http://redteamjournal.com/2009/01/red-teaming-criminal-insurgency-1/#more-711.

4. See John P. Sullivan and Adam Elkus, "State of Siege: Mexico's Criminal Insurgency," *Small Wars Journal*, August 2008.

5. See John P. Sullivan, "Transnational Gangs: The Impact of Third Generation Gangs in Central America," *Air & Space Power Journal* (Spanish Edition), Second Trimester 2008 at http://airpower.maxwell.af.mil.apjintrnational/apj-s/2008/2tri08/ sullivan eng.htm for a discussion of recent developments related to transnational gangs.

6. 'Hollow states' are defined by John Robb at his web blog *Global Guerrillas*; see http://globalguerrillas.typepad.com for his many discussions on this topic.

7. Samuel D. Porteous, "The Threat from Transnational Crime: An Intelligence Perspective," *Commentary* No. 70, Canadian Security Intelligence Service, Winter 1996.

8. Phil Williams, "The Nature of Drug-Trafficking Networks," *Current History*, Vol. 97, No. 618, April 1998, pp.154-159.

9. See John P. Sullivan and Keith Weston, "Afterward: Law Enforcement Response Strategies for Criminal-States and Criminal-Soldiers," in Robert J. Bunker (Ed.), *Criminal States and Criminal-Soldiers*, London: Routledge, 2008, pp. 287-300.

10. Robert J. Bunker and John P. Sullivan, "Cartel Evolution: Potentials and Consequences," *Transnational Organized Crime*, Vol. 4, No. 2, Summer 1998, pp. 55-74.

11. Ibid.

12. Ibid.

13. See John P. Sullivan, "Maras Morphing: Revisiting Third Generation Gangs," *Global Crime*, Vol.7, No. 3–4, August–November 2006, pp. 487-504 for a detailed discussion of the current state of maras and third generation (3 GEN) gangs worldwide.

14. John P. Sullivan, "Transnational Gangs: The Impact of Third Generation Gangs in Central America."

15. Cindy Franco, "The MS-13 and 18th Street Gangs: Emerging Transnational Gang Threats?" *CRS Report for Congress*, Washington, DC: Congressional Research Service (RL34233), 02 November 2007, p. 2.

16. John P. Sullivan, "Third Generation Street Gangs: Turf, Cartels, and Net Warriors," *Transnational Organized Crime*, Vol. 3, No. 3, Autumn 1997, pp. 95-108.

17. John P. Sullivan, "Urban Gangs Evolving as Criminal Netwar Actors," *Small Wars and Insurgencies*, Vol. 1, No.1, Spring 2000, pp. 82-96.

18. See John P. Sullivan, "Gangs Hooligans, and Anarchists—The Vanguard of Netwar in the Streets," in John Arquilla and David Ronfeldt, *Networks and Netwars: The Future of Terror, Crime, and Militancy*, Santa Monica: RAND, 2001, pp. 99-128 for a discussion of the analysis underlying this section.

19. Thomas C. Bruneau, "The Maras and National Security in Central America," *Strategic Insights*, Vol. IV, Issue 5 (May

2005) found at http://www.ccc.npps.navy.mil/si/2005/May/
bruneauMay05.pdf.

20. See John P. Sullivan and Adam Elkus, "Red Teaming
Criminal Insurgency" and "State of Siege: Mexico's Criminal
Insurgency." And John P. Sullivan, "Criminal Netwarriors in
Mexico's Drug Wars," *GroupIntel*, 22 December 2008 at http://
www.groupintel.com/2008/12/22/criminal-netwarriors-in-
mexico's-drug-wars/.

21. See John P. Sullivan, "The Missing Mission: Expeditionary
Police for Peacekeeping and Transnational Stability, *Small
Wars Journal*, 9 May 2008 at http://smallwarsjournal.com/
blog/2007/05/the-missing-mission-expedition/ and Doron
Zimmerman, "On the Future of Counter-terrorism Force
Development: The case for Third Force Options,'" unpublished
paper presented to the Panel on Patterns of Conflict: Future
Threat Analysis, International Studies Association, 50th ISA
Annual Convention, NY, NY, 18 February 2009.

22. John P. Sullivan, "Forging Improved Government Agency
Cooperation to Combat Violence, *National Strategy Forum
Review*, Vol., 17, No. 4, Fall 2008, pp. 24-29.

23. See John P. Sullivan, "Global Terrorism and the Police,"
unpublished paper presented to the Panel on Bridging
Divides in Counterterrorism Intelligence: Law Enforcement,
Intelligence, and Non-Traditional Actors, International Studies
Association, 49 th Annual ISA Convention, San Francisco,
CA, USA, 29 March 2008. See John P. Sullivan, "Terrorism
Early Warning and Co-Production of Counterterrorism
Intelligence," unpublished paper presented to Canadian
Association for Security and Intelligence Studies, CASIS
20th Anniversary Conference, Montreal, Quebec, Canada,
21 October 2005, available at http://www.projectwhitehorse.
com/pdfs/ 6.%20CASIS_Sullivan_paper1.pdf.

CHAPTER 5: THIRD-GENERATION GANGS AND CRIMINAL INSURGENCY IN LATIN AMERICA

1. Stephanie Hanson, "Brazil's Powerful Prison Gang," *Council
on Foreign Relations Backgrounder*, September 26, 2006, www.
cfr.org/publication/11542/; Samuel Logan, "Riots Reveal

Organized Crime Power in Brazil," *International Relations and Security Network*, May 18, 2006.

2. Ana Arana, "How the Street Gangs Took Central America," *Foreign Affairs*, May/June 2005, pp. 98-99.

3. On gangs in Central America, see Federico Brevé, "The Maras: A Menace to the Americas," *Military Review*, July 2007, pp. 91-92; Thomas Bruneau, "The Maras and National Security in Central America," *Strategic Insights*, May 2005, www.ccc.nps.navy.mil/si/2005/May/bruneauMay05.pdf; Clare Ribando Seelke, "Gangs in Central America," *Congressional Research Service Report*, October 17, 2008, passim.

4. As various authors have pointed out, a few groups—most notably the PCC—do profess an ideology based on economic redistribution and social justice. Given the fact that these gangs use brutal violence in dealing with the poor as well as the rich, however, it seems likely that such statements are merely justifications for criminal activity.

5. For a discussion of gang typologies, see John P. Sullivan, "Third Generation Street Gangs: Turf, Cartels, and Netwarriors," *Transnational Organized Crime* 3 (1997), pp. 95-108; idem, "Transnational Gangs: The Impact of Third Generation Gangs in Central America," *Air & Space Power Journal* (Spanish Edition), Second Trimester 2008, airpower.maxwell.af.mil.apjintrnational/apj-s/2008/2tri08/sullivan eng.htm.

6. Quoted in Moisés Naím, *Illicit: How Smugglers, Traffickers, and Copycats are Hijacking the Global Economy* (New York: Anchor Books, 2005), p. 36.

7. A good summary of the conditions conducive to third-generation gang activity can be found in Max Manwaring, *A Contemporary Challenge to State Sovereignty: Gangs and Other Illicit Transnational Criminal Organizations in Central America, El Salvador, Mexico, Jamaica, and Brazil* (Carlisle Barracks, PA: Strategic Studies Institute, 2007), passim; also Vanda Felbab-Brown, "Tackling Transnational Crime: Adapting U.S. National Security Policy," July 18, 2008, www.brookings.edu/articles/2008/ spring_latin_america_felbabbrown.aspx?p=1.

8. See Christopher Araujo, "Central America's Increasing Gang Problem," *Council on Hemispheric Affairs Report*, July 31,

2007, www.coha.org/2007/07/central-america%E2%80%99s-increasing-gang-problem-a-comfortinghandshake-needed-as-much-as-a-tough-fist-to-fight-crime-epidemic/.

9. On the PCC's international ties, see Logan, "Riots Reveal Organized Crime Power in Brazil."

10. National Drug Intelligence Center, *National Drug Threat Assessment 2008*, www.usdoj.gov/ndic/pubs25/25921/25921p.pdf; George Grayson, "Los Zetas: The Ruthless Army Spawned by a Mexican Drug Cartel," May 2008, www.fpri.org/enotes/200805.grayson.loszetas.html.

11. Steven Boraz and Thomas Bruneau, "Are the Maras Overwhelming Governments in Central America?" *Military Review*, November-December 2006, p. 37.

12. Grayson, "Los Zetas"; Colleen W. Cook, "Mexico's Drug Cartels," Congressional Research Service Report, October 16, 2007, p. 8.

13. Andrew Downie, "Brazil Gang Takes on State," *Christian Science Monitor*, May 16, 2006; Marcelo Soares, "Inmates Unleash a Torrent of Violence on Brazilian City," *Los Angeles Times*, May 16, 2006.

14. Grayson, "Los Zetas"; U.S. Agency for International Development, *Central America and Mexico Gang Assessment: Annex 2: Guatemala Profile*, April 2006, www.usaid.gov/gt/docs/guatemala_profile.pdf; Logan, "Riots Reveal Organized Crime Power in Brazil"; Joao de Barros, "Brazil's Real Overlords," Le Monde Diplomatique, January 25, 2007; Celinda Franco, "The MS-13 and 18 th Street Gangs: Emerging Transnational Gang Threats?" *Congressional Research Service Report*, January 30, 2008, pp. 8-9; Samuel Logan, "MS-13 Organization and U.S. Response," *Seguridad & democracia*, February 2007, www.samuellogan.com/publications/MS-13-Organizationand-US-Response.pdf.

15. USAID, *Central America and Mexico Gang Assessment: Annex 2: Guatemala Profile*; "Mexican Government Sends 6500 Troops to State Scarred by Drug Violence, Beheadings" International Herald Tribune, December 11, 2006; "Es provocación cabeza arrojada en alcaldia de Acapulco," La Crónica, June 30, 2006; Adam Elkus, "Gangs, Terrorists, and Trade," *Foreign*

Policy in Focus Report, April 12, 2007, http://www.fpif.org/fpiftxt/4144.

16. See Arana, "How the Street Gangs Took Central America," pp. 98-99.

17. William Langewiesche, "City of Fear,," *Vanity Fair*, April 2007, www.vanityfair.com/politics/features/2007/04/langewiesche200704; Telephone interview conducted by the author with a DEA official, July 23, 2008; Manwaring, *Contemporary Challenge to State Sovereignty*, pp. 27-29.

18. Jose de Cordoba and David Luhnow, "Mexican Officials Allege Drug Cartel Infiltrated Attorney General's Office," *Wall Street Journal*, October 28, 2008; Colleen Cook, "Mexico's Drug Cartels," *Congressional Research Service Report*, February 25, 2008, p. 9; "Drug Charges for Guatemala Tsar," BBC News, November 16, 2005; N.C. Aizenman, "Endurance of Corruption Shakes Guatemala Anew," *Washington Post*, March 11, 2006; Luis Esteban G. Manrique, "A Parallel Power: Organised Crime in Latin America," *Real Instituto Elcano de Estudios Internacionales y Estratégicos*, September 28, 2006, www.realinstitutoelcano.org/analisis/1049.asp.

19. Marc Lacey, "Killings in Drug War in Mexico Double in '08," New York Times, December 8, 2008; "Homicide Rates Highest in Southern Africa, Central and South America," *UN News Centre*, 30 December 2008, www.un.org/apps/news/story.asp?NewsID=29435&Cr=unodc&Cr1.

20. "Latin America Tops Murder Tables," *BBC News*, November 26, 2008, news.bbc.co.uk/2/hi/americas/7750054.stm.

21. George Grayson, "Surge Two," *Center for Immigration Studies Report*, October 27, 2008, www.frontpagemag.com/Articles/Read.aspx?GUID=3841DDDC-CF92-43EC-BB94-E1C071D31220.

22. Bureau for Latin American and Caribbean Affairs, *Central America and Mexico Gang Assessment* (Washington, D.C.: USAID, 2006), p. 20.

23. Bureau for Latin American and Caribbean Affairs, *Central America and Mexico Gang Assessment*, p. 9; see also Vanda Felbab-Brown, "Tackling Transnational Crime."

24. See Langewiesche, "City of Fear"; Ginger Thompson, "Shuttling Between Nations, Latino Gang Confound the

Law," *New York Times*, September 26, 2004; Freedom House, "Freedom in the World—El Salvador (2007)," www.freedomhouse.org/ inc/content/pubs/fiw/inc_country_detail.cfm?year=2007&country=7171&pf.

25. See Clare Ribando Seelke, "Anti-Gang Efforts in Central America: Moving Beyond Mano Dura?" *Report for the Maras, Security and Development in Central America Task Force*, April 10, 2007, www6.miami.edu/hemisphericpolicy/SeelkeTaskForcePaper.pdf, esp. pp. 3-4.

26. On existing U.S. programs, see Ribando Seelke, "Gangs in Central America," pp. 12-17.

27. On these programs, see USAID, *Central America and Mexico Gang Assessment*, pp. 13-14, 30-32; Laurence Iliff and Alfredo Corchado, "2 Mexican States Trying Out New Justice System," *Dallas Morning News*, August 18, 2008; Daniel Kurtz-Phelan, "The Long War of Genaro García Luna," *New York Times*, July 13, 2008; Julieta Palma and Raúl Urzúa, "Anti-Poverty Policies and Citizenry: The Chile Solidario Experience," Paris: UNESCO, 2005, unesdoc.unesco.org/images/0014/001402/140240e.pdf, pp.20-22.

CHAPTER 6: A VOLATILE BREW

1. This takes care of the (correct) observation that Hezbollah had been in SA previous to Chavez.

2. A reviewer asked that this be footnoted. In a previous article I used a piece by LTC Phillip Abbot, writing in *Military Review*, September-October 2004. But any cursory web search using "Cuidad del Este, Hezbollah al-Quada" or some similar formulation will turn up many references to Hezbollah's presence there, including testimony by U.S. state department officials.

3. A reviewer asked that some cities be named; this rewrite answers the mail and is smoother.

4. *CRS* report "Mexico's Drug Gangs," Feb 2008, p. 5.

5. I've already given a number for the trade, so this just says "billions."

6. I agree with cutting out the rest of the para, and have done so. But I disagree with the reviewer that "most of the people

who learned that lesson are now in the private sector." The government doesn't just run on political appointees, and even if that were not so, the present Administration seems to have taken the lessons to heart.

7. This is the near-unanimous opinion of U.S. law enforcement experts to whom I have talked; in fact, a source in LA believes there have already been attempts that were cartel operations. But rather than quote them by name, I'll just make it my own prediction.

CHAPTER 7: CARTEL V. CARTEL: MEXICO'S CRIMINAL INSURGENCY

1. Arthur Brice, "Deadliest Year in Mexico's War on Drugs," *CNN*, 1 January 2010, http://edition.cnn.com/2009/ WORLD/americas/12/31/mexico.violence/.

2. For a look at some recent example of cartel infighting, see Dane Schiller and Dudley Althaus, "Mexican drug cartels fight military and one another," *Houston Chronicle*, 16 December 2009, http://www.chron.com/disp/story.mpl/ metropolitan/6774555.html.

3. For a summary of the conflict so far, see the previous two pieces by Sullivan and Elkus in *Small Wars Journal*, "State of Siege: Mexico's Criminal Insurgency," Small Wars Journal, 19 August 2008, http://smallwarsjournal.com/blog/2008/08/ state-of-siege-mexicos-crimina/ and "Plazas for Profit: Mexico's Criminal Insurgency," 26 April 2009, http://smallwarsjournal. com/blog/2009/04/plazas-for-profit-mexicos-crim/. This piece is the third in an ongoing open-source effort by Sullivan and Elkus to track the strategic and operational dynamics of the Mexican criminal insurgency.

4. For a critique of such analytical tendencies, see Frank Hoffman, "Neoclassical Counterinsurgency," *Parameters*, Summer 2007, pp. 71-87. Also see Steven Metz, *Rethinking Insurgency*, Carlisle Barracks: Strategic Studies Institute, 2007. The works of historian Eric Hobswawm on "social banditry" are also of interest to the debate.

5. Mark T. Clark, "Does Clausewitz Apply to Criminal-States and Gangs" in Robert J. Bunker (Ed.), *Criminal States and*

Criminal Soldiers, New York: Routledge, 2008 explains how Clausewitz is still supremely relevant in analysis of sub-state violence.

6. There has been a substantial literature that has accumulated on the Mexican drug war. We recommend, in particular, David Danelo, "Disorder on the Border" in U.S. *Naval Institute Proceedings*, October 2009, http://www.usni.org/magazines/proceedings/story.asp?STORY_ID=2055; Hal Brands, *Mexico's NarcoInsurgency and U.S. Counter-Drug Policy*, Carlisle Barracks: Strategic Studies Institute, May 2009; and Fernan Celaya Pacheco, "Narcofearance: How has Narcoterrorism Settled in Mexico?" *Studies in Conflict & Terrorism*, Volume 32, Issue 12, December 2009, pp.1021–1048.

7. For a general history of Mexico that explains the context of political violence and corruption, see Enrique Krauze, *Mexico, Biography of Power: A History of Modern Mexico 1810- 1996*, New York: Harper Perennial, 1998.

8. Alfred Corchado, "Slums are Front Lines in Mexico's Drug War," *Dallas Morning News*, 1 January 2010. http://www.dallasnews.com/sharedcontent/dws/ news/world/mexico/stories/DN- barrio_01int.ART.State.Edition2.4b9fac8.html.

9. Hector Berrera, "Slain El Monte School-Board Member Bobby Salcedo is Honored, Mourned," *Los Angeles Times*, 4 January 2010, http://www.latimes.com/news/local/la-me-el-monte5-2010jan05,0,7990747.story.

10. Samuel Logan, "Los Zetas: Evolution of a Criminal Organization," *ISN Security Watch*, 11 March 2009, http://www.isn.ethz.ch/isn/Current-Affairs/Security-Watch/Detail/?id=97554&lng=en.

11. See Philip Caputo, "The Fall of Mexico," *The Atlantic*, December 2009, http://www.theatlantic.com/doc/200912/mexico-drugs.

12. José de Cordoba and Joel Millman, "Mexico Ramps Up Drug War With a Surge on Rio Grande," *Wall Street Journal*, 22 December 2009, http://online.wsj.com/ article/SB126143123803700665.html.

13. Juan David Leal, "Retan narcos a soldados como si fueran otro ejército: analistas," *El Diario*, 9 December 2009, http://

Mexico's Criminal Insurgency

www.diario.com.mx/nota.php?notaid=8414ff5be4872395a7f
fc85accc7d1a4.

14. "7,724 Slain in Mexico in 2009," *Latin American Herald Tribune*, 2 January 2010, http://www.laht.com/article.asp?ArticleId=349667&CategoryId=14091.

15. José de Cordoba and Joel Millman, "Mexico Ramps Up Drug War With a Surge on Rio Grande."

16. Ibid.

17. Tracy Wilkinson, "Rights group faults Mexico over alleged army abuse," *Los Angeles Times*, 9 December 2009; Amy Isackson, "Amnesty International Urges Mexico To Investigate Tijuana Torture Claims," *KPBS News*, 8 December 2009, and *Mexico: New Reports of Human Rights Violations by the Military*, London: Amnesty International, AMR 41/058/2009, December 2009, http://www.amnesty.org/en/library/asset/AMR41/058/2009/en/e1a94ad6-3df1-a5454724f0b93f39af69/amr410582009en.pdf.

18. Amy Isackson, "Fighting Common Crime A Priority In Tijuana This Year," *KPBS News*, January 2010, http://www.kpbs.org/news/2010/jan/05/fighting-common-crime-priority-tij.

19. Julian Cardona, "Mexico army hands control to police in drug war city," *Reuters*, 15 January 2010, http://ca.reuters.com/article/topNews/ idCATRE60F0DB2010016.

20. See John P. Sullivan, "Police-Military Interaction in Mexico's Drug War," *Air & Space Power Journal-Spanish Edition*, Third Trimester 2009, http://www.airpower.au.af.mil/apjinternational/apj-s/2009/3tri09/sullivaneng.htm for a discussion of the complexities and challenges of integrating police and military operations countering high intensity crime and criminal insurgency in Mexico.

21. Robin Emmett, "Mexico Turns to Navy to Bolster Flagging Drug War," Reuters, 18 December 2009, http://www.reuters.com/article/ idUSTRE5BH4CF20091218.

22. Elizabeth Malkin, "Revenge in Drug War Chills Mexico," 22 December 2009, http://www.nytimes.com/2009/12/23/world/americas/23mexico.html?_ .

23. Víctor Ballinas, "'Ni tregua ni cuartel para los enemigos de la patria', advierte Felipe Calderón," *La Jornada*, 22 December

2009, http://www.jornada.unam.mx/2009/12/22/ index.php ?section=politica&article=006n1pol.

24. See "Asume Héctor Beltrán el mando del cártel: Policía Federal," Noroeste.com, 4 January 2010, http://www.noroeste. com.mx/publicaciones. php?id=544822.

25. Ramon Bracamontes, "No Quick Fix Seen for Drug Battle in Juárez," *El Paso Times*, 27 December 2009, http://www. elpasotimes.com/ ci_14074596?source=most_viewed.

26. "Se reagupa hampa en México en dos megacarteles," *Imagen del Golfo*, 26 January 2010, http://www.imagendelgolfo.com. mx/resumen.php?id=151629.

27. "El Teo," Teodoro Garcia Simental was arrested Tuesday, 12 January 2010 in La Paz, Baja California. The vacuum created by Garcia's arrest is expected to fuel even more violence. El Teo is accused of dissolving victims in barrels of lye and waging a terror campaign that turned Tijuana into one of Mexico's most dangerous cities. See Martha Mendoza and Elliot Spagat, "Violence expected as Mexican drug lord arrested," *Washington Post*, 13 January 2010 and Richard Marosi and Ken Ellingwood, "Mexican drug lord Teodoro Garcia Simental, known for his savagery, is captured," *Los Angeles Times*, 13 January 2010 for details on this barbaric leader of one of the Tijuana cartel's factions.

28. Jason Buch, "South Texan may be the next drug king," *San Antonio Express-News*, 24 January 2010, http://www. mysanantonio.com/news/mexico/82535092 .html.

29. Ken Ellingwood, "Book Takes Mexican Drug War to Task," *Los Angeles Times*, 1 January 2009. http://www.latimes.com/news/ nation-and-world/la-fg-narco-book1-2010jan01,0,6239821. story.

30. Brands, p. 33.

31. Brands, p. 36.

32. Brands, p. 37.

33. Brands, p. 39.

CHAPTER 8:
CRIMINAL INSURGENCIES IN THE AMERICAS

No notes.

CHAPTER 9: THE SPIRITUAL
SIGNIFICANCE OF ¿PLATA O PLOMO?

a. Typo from initial publication corrected from 2005 to 2006 date.
1. Background works include Robert J. Bunker and John P. Sullivan, "Cartel Evolution: Potentials and Consequences." *Transnational Organized Crime.* Vol. 2, No. 2, 1998, pp. 55-74; John P. Sullivan and Adam Elkus, "State of Siege: Mexico's Criminal Insurgency." *Small Wars Journal.* August 2008, pp. 1-12; Hal Brands, Mexico's Narco-Insurgency and U.S. CounterDrug Policy. Carlisle: Strategic Studies Institute, US Army War College, 2009; and Max G. Manwaring, *A "New" Dynamic in the Western Hemisphere Security Environment: The Mexican Zetas and Other Private Armies.* Carlisle: Strategic Studies Institute, US Army War College, 2009.
2. See Ralph Peters, "The New Warrior Class." Parameters. Vol. 24, No. 2. Summer 1994, pp. 16-26; and Martin van Creveld, *The Transformation of War.* New York: The Free Press, 1991.
3. Robert J. Bunker, ed. *Narcos Over the Border: Gangs, Cartels and Mercenaries.* London: Routledge, 2011. Initially published as a special issue of *Small Wars & Insurgencies*, Vol. 21, No. 1. These spiritual insights represent an extension of some of the conclusions drawn in a chapter by Pamela L. Bunker, Lisa J. Campbell, and Robert J. Bunker on "Torture, beheadings, and narcocultos."
4. Max G. Manwaring, *Insurgency, Terrorism & Crime.* Norman: University of Oklahoma Press, 2008, pp. 116-118.

CHAPTER 10: EXPLOSIVE ESCALATION?
REFLECTIONS ON THE CAR BOMBING IN CIUDAD
JUAREZ

1. See John P. Sullivan and Adam Elkus, "State of Siege: Mexico's Criminal Insurgency," *Small Wars Journal*, 19 August 2008, http://smallwarsjournal.com/blog/2008/08/state-of-siege-mexicos-crimina/; "Plazas for Profit: Mexico's Criminal Insurgency," *Small Wars Journal*, 26 April 2009, http://smallwarsjournal.com/blog/2009/04/plazas-for-profit-

mexicos-crim/; and "Cartel v. Cartel: Mexico'Criminal Insurgency," *Small Wars Journal*, 1 February 2010, http://smallwarsjournal.com/blog/2010/02/cartel-vcartel-mexicos-crimin/ for a view of the trajectory of Mexico's narco-conflict.

2. Alicia A. Caldwell, "US official: Mexican car bomb likely used Tovex," *Associated Press*, 19 July 2010, http://www.google.com/hostednews/ap/article/ALeqM5gMi5B2USfJStXxfqgWWr2xjRYpOgD9H2FA2G0.

3. See Mike Davis, *Buda's Wagon: A Brief History of the Car Bomb*, New York: Verso, 2007.

4. Alicia A. Caldwell and E. Eduardo Castillo, "Car bomb signals new dimension to Mexican drug war," *Associated Press*, 16 July 2010, http://news.yahoo.com/s/ap/ 20100716/ap_on_re_la_am_ca/lt_drug.

5. Alicia A. Caldwell and Alexandra Olsen, "Car bomb in Mexican drug war changes ground rules," *Associated Press*, 17 July 2010, http://www.google.com/hostednews/ap/article/ALeqM5gMi5B2USfJStXxfqgWWr2xjRYpOgD9H12AUG0.

6. "FACTBOX-Worst attacks in Mexico's drug war," *Reuters*, 18 July 2010, http://www.alertnet.org/thenews/newsdesk/N18131453.htm.

7. Nick Miroff and William Booth, "Mexican drug cartels' newest weapon: Cold War-era grenades made in U.S.," *Washington Post*, 17 July 2010, http://www.washingtonpost.com/wpdyn/content/article/2010/07/16/AR2010071606252.html.

8. "Graffiti message warns of more violence in Juarez," *CNN News*, 19 July 2010, http://edition.cnn.com/2010/WORLD/americas/07/19/mexico.juarez.

9. See John P. Sullivan and Adam Elkus, "Red Teaming Criminal Insurgency," *Red Team Journal*, 30 January 2009, http://redteamjournal.com/2009/01/red-teaming-criminal-insurgency-1/.

10. See Christopher Flaherty, "3D tactics: an advanced warfare concept in critical infrastructure protection," *International Journal of Emergency Management*, Volume 4, Number 1, 2007 and "A New Approach to Mass Space," *Red Team Journal*, 12 July 2009, http://redteamjournal.com/2009/07/a-new-approach-to-mass-space/ for discussions related to the urban

situational awareness regarding attacks that can come from any number of directions and modes.

11. See for example, John P. Sullivan and Adam Elkus, "Beyond Active Response: An Operational Concept for Police Counterterrorism Response," *New Criminologist*, 14 May 2010, http://www.newcriminologist.com/article.asp?nid=2211 .

12. See John P. Sullivan, "The Missing Mission: Expeditionary Police for Peacekeeping and Transnational Stability," *Small Wars Journal*, 9 May 2007, http://smallwarsjournal.com/blog/2007/05/the-missing-mission-expedition/.

13. See John P. Sullivan, "Criminal Insurgency in the Americas," *Small Wars Journal*, 13 February 2010, http://smallwarsjournal.com/blog/2010/02/criminal-insurgency-in-america/.

14. See Adam Higginbottom, "State of the Art," *Wired*, August 2010, p. 138-144 for a discussion on IEDs in America's current expeditionary operations in Afghanistan and Iraq. Lest the reader feel the IED threat is overblown or is a concern only abroad and won't happen in the US recall the Times Square bomber's improvised explosive cum incendiary device in May 2010 and presence of IEDs at the Columbine massacre.

CHAPTER 11: THE US STRATEGIC IMPERATIVE MUST SHIFT FROM IRAQ/AFGHANISTAN TO MEXICO/THE AMERICAS AND THE STABILIZATION OF EUROPE

1. The initial usage of the term 'criminal insurgencies' is attributed to John P. Sullivan, a friend, scholar in his own right, and frequent co-writer of essays on gang and cartel issues. The term has proven to be an excellent fit to describe 'blurred crime and war' / 'gray area' conflict between states and non-state organizations within the more encompassing Epochal Warfare paradigm.

CHAPTER 12: CRIMINAL INSURGENCIES IN MEXICO: WEB AND SOCIAL MEDIA RESOURCES

1. From January through November 2010, a total of 12,456 killings took place. See Jens Erik Gould and Thomas Black, "Mexico Drug War Death Toll Climbs to 30,196 Since 2006,

Government Says". *Bloomberg.* December 16, 2010, http://www.bloomberg.com/news/2010-12-16/mexico-drug-war-death-toll-climbs-to-30-196since-2006-government-says.html (Accessed 31 December 2010).

2. Tracy Wilkinson and Ken Ellingwood, "Mexico army no match for drug cartels". *Los Angeles Times.* Thursday, December 30, 2010: A1, A6. Online version variant; http://articles.latimes.com/2010/dec/29/world/la-fg-mexico-army-20101230 (Accessed 31 December 2010).

3. Associated Press (Guatemala City), "Drug gang suspects threaten 'war' in Guatemala". December 28, 2010, http://www.forbes.com/feeds/ap/2010/12/28/general-lt-drug-warguatemala_8227446.html?boxes=financechannelAP (Accessed 31 December 2010).

4. Alfredo Corchado, "Obama condemns U.S. consulate killings in Mexico". *The Dallas Morning News.* Monday, March 15, 2010, http://www.dallasnews.com/sharedcontent/dws/dn/latestnews/stories/031410dnintmexicoconsulate.1a8bdb848.html (Accessed 3 January 2011).

5. This perception is in variance to the primacy of current U.S. foreign and defense policies focused on eliminating the Al Qaeda and Taliban enclaves in Afghanistan and Western Pakistan, stabilizing that nation as a fledgling democracy, and eliminating Al Qaeda influence in Iraq and bringing about some sort of democratic covenant between the competing Sunni, Shia, and Kuridish populations so that Iraq does not fragment into three smaller sovereign entities. Where higher stakes do exist is with the security of the nuclear weapons and materials in Pakistan—all agree that Al Qaeda and affinity group access to such weapons and materials would likely see them used against Western Europe or the United States.

6. Will Weissert, "Countless Juarez residents flee 'dying city'". Associated Press. Wednesday 29 December 2010, http://www.msnbc.msn.com/id/40844625/ns/world_news-americas/ (Accessed 31 December 2010). Information on vacant and abandoned homes provided by a source to one of the authors on a non-attribution basis at a Trans-Border Institute (TBI), University of San Diego, invitation-only roundtable on 'Drug

Trafficking, Violence, and Public Security in Mexico' on December 10, 2010.

7. Associated Press, "Mexico Cartels Empty Border Towns." Saturday, April 17, 2010, http://www.borderlandbeat. com/2010/04/mexico-cartels-empty-border-towns.html (Accessed 31 December 2010).

8. Mark Stevenson, "Residents not returning to town hit by Mexico drug war." Associated Press. November 23, 2010, http://www.msnbc.msn.com/id/40321769/ns /world_news-americas/ (Accessed 31 December 2010).

9. Information operations (info ops) aimed at securing freedom to operate are an increasingly important element of the drug war. See John P. Sullivan, "Cartel Info Ops: Power and Counterpower in Mexico's Drug War," *MountainRunner* (www.MountainRunner.us), 15 November 2010, for a discussion of this dimension.

10. Tracy Wilkinson, "Caught behind enemy lines,' *Los Angeles Times*, 6 November 2010, http://articles.latimes.com/2010/ nov/06/world/la-fg-mexico-cartel-rule-20101106 (Accessed 9 January 2011).

11. Ibid.

12. See Hal Brands, "Third-Generation Gangs and Criminal Insurgency in Latin America," *Small Wars Journal*, 4 July 2009, http://smallwarsjournal.com/blog/2009 /07/thirdgeneration-gangsand-crim/; John P. Sullivan, "Criminal Insurgency in the Americas," *Small Wars Journal*, 13 February 2010, http:// smallwarsjournal.com/blog/2010/02/criminal-insurgency-in-america/; and Max G. Manwaring, *A Contemporary Challenge to State Sovereignty: Gangs and Other Illicit Transnational Criminal Organizations (TCOs) in Central America, El Salvador, Mexico, Jamaica, and Brazil*, Carlisle, PA: Strategic Studies Institute, 2008 at http://www.strategicstudiesinstitute. army.mil/pubs/display.cfm?pubID=837 fordiscussion of the now and future prospects for criminal insurgencies in Latin America.

CHAPTER 13: THE MEXICAN CARTEL DEBATE: AS VIEWED THROUGH FIVE DIVERGENT FIELDS OF SECURITY STUDIES

1. Key authors may write and have influence in more than one field of study. They have been assigned to the field of security studies which best characterizes their dominant works and impact. Note that some of the authors designated may have great impact in their field of studies but at present have not fully weighed in on the Mexican cartel debate. For omissions and errors made, I apologize.

2. John M. Hagedorn, *A World of Gangs*. Minneapolis, MN: University of Minnesota Press, 2008: 134.

3. This well known refrain is attributed to Brian Jenkins.

4. *Small Wars Journal* readers will benefit from this discussion because ultimately many of those readers either have an interest in, or actively identify themselves, with the field of insurgency (small wars) studies. That field of security studies, like the others, seeks to influence the Mexican cartel debate and this author would, among others, argue that the "insurgency" construct, albeit a criminal (as in John Sullivan's 'criminal insurgencies' construct) rather than a traditional political or revolutionary derived one, represents the most accurate perceptual lens by which to understand and respond to this threat—one that is in actuality grand strategic in nature.

5. Worst case scenarios for each of these fields of security studies may be different than projections of alternative futures. See Robert J. Bunker and John P. Sullivan, "Cartel evolution revisited: third phase cartel potentials and alternative futures in Mexico." Robert J. Bunker, ed., *Narcos Over the Border: Gangs, Cartels and Mercenaries*. London: Routledge, 2011: 46-50. Another future discussed is that of Mexico becoming a failed-state. For an analysis of state disintegration in Mexico see George W. Grayson, *Mexico: Narco-Violence and a Failed State?* New Brunswick, NJ: Transaction Publishers, 2010.

6. Matthew D. LaPlante, "Army Official Suggests U.S. Troops Might be Needed in Mexico." *The Salt Lake Tribune*. 8 February 2011 (Update), http://www.sltrib.com/sltrib/

home/5120768176/mexico-westphal-army-drug.html.csp#
(Accessed 9 February 2011).

7.   William Booth and Nick Miroff, "Mexican drug cartels draws
     Guatemalan army to jungles where it fought civil war." *The
     Washington Post*. 9 February 2011, http://www.washingtonpost.
     com/wp-dyn/content/article/2011/02/09 /AR2011020906371.
     html (Accessed 10 February 2011).

8.   Robert J. Bunker, "Strategic threat: narcos and narcotics
     overview." Robert J. Bunker, ed., *Narcos Over the Border:
     Gangs, Cartels and Mercenaries*. London: Routledge, 2011:
     21-24.

CHAPTER 14: ATTACKS ON JOURNALISTS AND "NEW MEDIA" IN MEXICO'S DRUG WAR: A POWER AND COUNTER POWER ASSESSMENT

1.   Information operations (informally known as "info ops")
     describes the military concept (doctrine) of shaping the
     battlespace through propaganda, access, control, surety, and
     denial of information.

2.   Media accounts of cartel killings range from 28,000-30,000
     killed since 2006. The *Los Angeles Times* tally counts 28,228
     persons killed as of 15 December 2010 based on Trans-Border
     Institute analysis of data from the *Reforma* newspaper.

References:

Campbell, H. (2009). *Drug War Zone*, Frontline Dispatches from the
     Streets of El Paso and Juárez, Austin; University of Texas Press.
Castells, M. (2007). "Communication, Power and Counter-power in
     the Network Society." International Journal of Communication.
     1: 238-266.
Committee to Protect Journalists (2010). Silence or Death in Mexico's
     Press.
El Diario (2010). ¿Qué quieren de nosotros?, Editorial, September 18
     at http://www.diario.com.mx/notas.php?f=2010/09/18&id=6b12
     4801376ce134c7d6ce2c7fb8fe2f. Translated at *Los Angeles Times*,
     La Plaza, 24 September 2010.

Fundación MEPI (2010). "México: La nueva espiral del silencio," 17 November at http://fundacionmepi.org/narco-violencia.html.

Grillo, I. (2010). Journalist, Mexico City, Personal communications, e-interview, 16 December.

IAPA, Inter American Press Association (2010). Statement of the IAPA General Assembly, November 5-9 2010, Mérida, Mexico.

Knight Center for Journalism in the Americas (2010). Google Maps/ Knight Center Map of Threats Against Journalists in Mexico. Austin: University of Texas; http://maps.google.com/maps/ms?ie= UTF8&hl=en&msa=0&z=6&msid=103960216204540664660.0 0048f4d72b6a3a226539 and http://knightcenter.utexas.edu/blog/ new-knight-center-map-pinpoints-threats-against-journalism-mexico.

McCombs, M. and Shaw, D.L. (1972). "The agenda setting function of the mass media," Public Opinion Quarterly, 36, pp. 176-185.

Medel, M. (2010). Journalism in Times of Threats, Censorship and Violence, Report from the Seminar "Cross-border Coverage of U.S.-Mexico Drug Trafficking," conducted March 26-27, 2010 at the Knight Center for Journalism in the Americas at the University of Texas at Austin, sponsored by the McCormick Foundation.

Grayson, G.W. (2010). Mexico: Narco-Violence and a Failed State?, New Brunswick: Transaction Publishers.

Hobsbawm, E. (1969). Bandits, New York: The New Press.

O'Connor, M. (2010). "Analysis: A PR department for Mexico's narcos," GlobalPost, 05 November at http://www.globalpost.com/dispatch/ worldview/101026/mexico-drug-war-cartels-newspapers.

O'Reilly, A. (2010). "Journalists Are Major Targets in Mexico's Drug War; Bloggers Use Twitter To Report," Latin America News Dispatch, 27 September at http://latindispatch.com/2010/09/27/ journalists-are-major-targets-in-mexicos-drug-war-bloggers-use-twitter-to-report/.

Rosales, C. (2010). News Editor, El Paso, Personal communication, e-interview, 15 December.

Terrence E. (Terry) Poppa (1990, 2010). Drug Lord: the Life and Death of a Mexican Kingpin, El Paso: Cinco Puntos Press.

Poppa, T. (2010). Author of Drug Lord, Telephonic interview, 01 November.

Sullivan and Elkus, E. (2010). "Cartel v. Cartel: Mexico's Criminal Insurgency, Small Wars Journal, February.

Trans-Border Institute (2010). Drug Violence in Mexico: Data and Analysis from 2001-2009. San Diego: University of San Diego, Joan Kroc School of Peace Studies.

Trans-Border Institute (2010). "Number of Drug Killings' in Mexico: January-June 2010," Crime Indicator Database for the Justice in Mexico Project at the Trans-Border Institute. San Diego: University of San Diego, Joan Kroc School of Peace Studies.

Tuckman, J. (2010). "Twitter feeds and blogs tell hidden story of Mexico's drug wars, The Guardian, 26 September.

Wilkinson, T. (2010). "Caught behind enemy lines," Los Angeles Times, 06 November.

CHAPTER 15: EXTREME BABARISM, A DEATH CULT, AND HOLY WARRIORS IN MEXICO: *SOCIETAL WARFARE SOUTH OF THE BORDER?*

a. Changed to red battle flag from white battle flag (typo in original).

1. "Book Review: Narcos Over the Border by Robert J. Bunker (Ed.)" *zenpundit.com.* 5 April 2011. http://zenpundit.com/?p=3870.

2. Her conclusions are that "Some gangs – the institutionalized and very violent – may in fact share characteristics with insurgencies, and thus the conflict lens and armed group framework might apply. But very few gangs reach this level, suggesting that such an approach is neither appropriate nor useful for understanding the thousands of gangs that exist in communities across the globe" (p. 386). Jennifer M. Hazen, "Understanding gangs as armed groups." *International Review of the Red Cross.* Vol. 92, No. 878. June 2010: 369-386. While these conclusions are indicative of the basic 'American street gang' derived from studies conducted by Thrasher, Klein, Maxson, and others they have nothing to do with the reality of armed gangs that operate in Mexico, Central America, Colombia, Brazil, Sierra Leone, and increasingly in many other regions of the Globe.

3. Both authors have numerous *Small Wars Journal* publications on what is taking place in Mexico. These include; "The Mexican Cartel Debate: As Viewed Through Five Divergent

Fields of Security Studies," "Criminal Insurgencies in Mexico: Web and Social Media Resources" and "Criminal Insurgency in the Americas."

4. See http://www.borderlandbeat.com/2011/03/narco-execution-videos-and-its-effects.html.

5. John P. Sullivan and Samuel Logan, "Los Zetas: Massacres, Assassinations and Infantry Tactics". *Homeland1.com*. 24 November 2010. http://www.homeland1.com/domestic-international-terrorism/articles/913612-Los-Zetas-Massacres-Assassinations-and-Infantry-Tactics/.

6. The original report is in Spanish and was published in *Milenio*. See *Borderland Beat*, "Study: 98.5% of Crimes Go Unpunished in Mexico." Saturday, 13 November 2010. http://www.borderlandbeat.com/2010/11/study-985-of-crimes-go-unpunished-in.html.

7. Associated Press, "Mexico Drug War Displaces 230,000 and Half Find Refuge in the U.S., Says Report." *Fox News*. 25 March 2011. http://latino.foxnews.com/latino/news/2011/03/25/report-mexico-drug-war-displaces-230000-half-refuge/.

8. Our analysis is based on Pamela L. Bunker, Lisa J. Campbell, and Robert J. Bunker, "Torture, beheadings, and narcocultos." *Small Wars & Insurgencies*. Vol. 21., No.1. March 2010: 165-169; *Noticieros Televisa*, "Identifican cabeza 'ofrendada' en tumba de 'El Barbas'." 18 January 2010. http://www2.esmas.com/noticierostelevisa/mexico/estados/130952/identifican-cabeza-abandonada-tumba-el-barbas; and on other English and Spanish sources including some incident photos and altar images. Useful background resources were Tony M. Kail, *Magico-Religious Groups and Ritualistic Activities: A Guide for First Responders*. Boca Raton, FL: CRC Press, 2008 and Tony Kail, *Santa Muerte: Mexico's Mysterious Saint of Death*. La Vergne, TN: Fringe Research Press, 2010.

9. For information on the 'Satanic panic' scare see some of the works highlighted in Robert J. Bunker and Pamela L. Bunker, *Subject Bibliography: Beheadings & Ritualized Murders*. FBI Academy Library, Quantico, VA: August 2007. http://fbilibrary.fbiacademy.edu/bibliographies/beheadings&ritualmurders.htm.

10. Claudia Bolaños, "Detienen a líder de Iglesia de la Santa Muerte." *El Universal*. 4 Martes 2011. http://www/eluniversal.com.mx/notas/734953.html.

11. Frank Main and Kim Janssen, "Sources: Two charged in double murder suspected in 10 other killings." Chicago *Sun-Times*. 2 April 2011. http://www.suntimes.com/4054640-417/sources-two-charged-in-double-murder-suspected-in-10-other-killings.html; and *El Diaro*, "Atribuyen crimen de menor a promesas hechas a Santa Muerte." 10 January 2011. http://www.diario.com.mx/notas.php?f=2011/01/10&id=1cc7002c4dd7445755dcfbe8662e081a.

12. Alfredo Corchado, "Drug cartels taking over government roles in parts of Mexico." *The Dallas Morning News*. 30 April 2011. http://www.dallasnews.com/news/state/headlines/20110430-drug-cartels-taking-over-government-roles-in-parts-of-mexico.ece.

13. George W. Grayson, "E-Notes: La Familia: Another Mexican Deadly Syndicate." Foreign Policy Research Institute. February 2009. http://www.fpri.org/enotes/200901.grayson.lafamilia.html.

14. Samuel Logan and John P. Sullivan, "Mexican Crime 'Family' is Cloaked in 'Divine Justice'." *Mexidata.info*. Monday, August 24, 2009. http://mexidata.info/id2378.html.

15. Associated Press, "Drug cartel stitches victim's face on soccer ball." *Msnbc.com*. 8 January 2010. http://www.msnbc.msn.com/id/34774234/ns/world_news-americas/t/drug-cartel-stitches-victims-face-soccer-ball/.

16. George W. Grayson, *La Familia Drug Cartel*. Carlisle, PA: Strategic Studies Institute, US Army War College, December 2010: 47.

17. Hannah Stone, "New Cartel Announces Takeover from Familia Michoacana." *In Sight*. Monday, 14 March 2011. http://www.insightcrime.org/insight-latest-news/item/671-new-cartel-announces-take-over-from-familia-michoacana.

18. Ibid.

19. We are not the only concerned observers. See Alma Guillermoprieto, "Days of the Dead: The new narcocultura," *The New Yorker*, 10 November 2008 for an excellent analysis by an eminent Mexican journalist of these potentials at

http://newyorker.com/reporting/2008/11/10/08111fact_
guillermprieto.

AFTERWORD:
MEXICO: A MOSAIC CARTEL WAR

1. Hal Brands, Mexico's Narco-Insurgency and US Counterdurg Policy, (Carlisle Barracks: Strategic Studies Institute, May 2009), 11.
2. Ed Vulliamy, "Killing for Kudos", *The Guardian online*, 7 February 2010, http://www.guardian.co.uk/world/2010/feb/07/mexico-drug-war (accessed on 5 July 2010).
3. Jorg Raab and H. Brinton Milward, "Dark Networks as Problems", *Journal of Public Administration Research and Theory*, (October 2003).
4. Vadim Volkov, *Violent Entrepreneurs*, (Ithaca: Cornell University Press, 2002), 27-28.
5. Diego Gambetta, *The Sicilian Mafia*, (Cambridge: Harvard University Press), 2.

NOTES ON CONTRIBUTORS

Primary Authors

John P. Sullivan, Senior Fellow with *SWJ El Centro*, is a career police officer. He currently serves as a lieutenant with the Los Angeles Sheriff's Department. He is also a Senior Research Fellow at the Center for Advanced Studies on Terrorism (CAST) and Adjunct Researcher at the Scientific Vortex Foundation in Bogotá, Colombia. His current research focus is the impact of transnational organized crime on sovereignty in Mexico and elsewhere. Collaborative works include *Global Biosecurity: Threats and Responses* (Routledge, 2010) and *Countering Terrorism and WMD: Creating a Global Counter-Terrorism Network* (Routledge, 2006).

Dr. Robert J. Bunker, Senior Fellow with *SWJ El Centro*, is a past senior officer of the Counter-OPFOR Corporation. He is currently adjunct faculty with the School of Politics and Economics, Claremont Graduate University and an instructor with the Los Angeles High Intensity Drug Trafficking Area (LA HIDTA). He has over two hundred publications, including edited and co-authored books, and specializes in terrorism, homeland security, and international security. Collaborative works include *Criminal Insurgencies in Mexico and the Americas* (Routledge, 2012), *Narcos Over the Border* (Routledge, 2011), *Criminal-States and Criminal-Soldiers* (Routledge, 2008), and *Networks, Terrorism, and Global Insurgency* (Routledge, 2005).

Contributing Authors

Dr. Hal Brands, Fellow with *SWJ El Centro*, is Assistant Professor of Public Policy at Duke University. He is the author of *Latin America's Cold War* (Harvard Press, 2010), and *From Berlin to Baghdad: America's Search for Purpose in the Post-Cold War World* (Kentucky Press, 2008). He has written several studies on Latin American security issues for the Department of the Army, the Department of Defense, and SOUTHCOM.

Pamela L. Bunker, a *SWJ* contributor, is a past senior officer of the Counter-OPFOR Corporation. She graduated from California State Polytechnic University Pomona with a B.S. in anthropology/geography and a B.S. in social science and from The Claremont Graduate University with a M.A. in public policy with additional post-graduate work completed in comparative politics and government. Specializations include non-state threat and fringe/radicalized groups.

Dave Dilegge, Editor-in-Chief of *SWJ*, is a retired Marine Corps Reserve officer and independent defense consultant who specializes in irregular warfare and urban operations. He was the primary author of DOD's *Urban Generic Intelligence Requirements Handbook* and *North Korea Handbook* and was the project lead on a USMC initiative that conducted interviews of Chechen Commanders concerning urban operations against Russian forces. He also serves as a Director on the Small Wars Foundation's Board of Directors.

Adam Elkus, Associate with *SWJ El Centro*, is an analyst specializing in foreign policy and security. He is currently Editor of *Red Team Journal*. His articles have been published in *The Atlantic, Small Wars Journal, The Huffington Post, Defense Concepts*, and related publications. He blogs at *Rethinking Security*.

Dr. Paul Rexton Kan, Fellow with *SWJ El Centro*, is currently an Associate Professor of National Security Studies and the Henry L. Stimson Chair of Military Studies at the US Army War College. He is also the author of the book *Drugs and Contemporary Warfare* (Potomac Books 2009). He recently completed field research along the US-Mexico border for his forthcoming book, *Cartels at War: Mexico's Drug Fueled Violence and the Threat to US National Security* (Potomac Books).

Col. Robert Killebrew (U.S. Army, retired), Fellow with *SWJ El Centro*, is a private consultant in national defense issues. He is a retired Army infantry colonel with service in U.S. Army Special Forces and airborne units, and he has taught national and military strategy at the Army War College. He is a Non-Resident Senior Fellow with the Center for a New American Security and co-author of *Crime Wars; Gangs, Cartels and U.S. National Security* (CNAS, 2010).

Dr. Max G. Manwaring, is a Professor of Military Strategy at the U.S. Army War College, a retired Army Colonel, and a Ph.D. from the University of Illinois. He writes extensively on violent non-state actors such as insurgents, gangs, transnational criminal organizations, and private armies. His most recent article is "Three Lessons from Contemporary Challenges to Security," *PRISM*, June 2011. His most recent book is *Gangs, Pseudo Militias, and other Modern Mercenaries: New Dynamics in Uncomfortable Wars* (University of Oklahoma Press, 2010).